The Eighty-Eight

Collis

Cover Art by Blaine Prescott

ISBN: 0996976248
ISBN-13: 978-0996976244

ACKNOWLEDGMENTS

Special thanks to Josiah for all the support and belief; and to Tom for pulling my work into the light of day.

"Monsters" first appeared in Flash Fiction Magazine, 2015

CONTENTS

1. Genes of Is

Two bodies joined to become one. He pressed into her and she pressed fully back. Moving up and down, in and out, forward and back like the tide. Legs and arms everywhere, intertwined and wrapping. Their salty sweat became the ocean they swam in. Four arms and four legs, at once a human octopus. With their camouflage white under the covers, they had no predators in the world save each other.

The birth, the beginning, the being. Some say with no humor, the continuing. Still others moan; nothing. Never was nothing. Never will be nothing. The crowning achievement, the crown breaks the light. In a mud hut 300 hundred years past in West Africa. In a Midwest hospital with white sterile walls and mutant bacteria covering everything else. In a crowded Martian city 2000 years from now. And in the snow blocks of an Eskimo igloo in the far north five thousand years past. Since the beginning, until the end. The eye is once again closed, as two freshly open. To the doctor, the mother, the happy world. What will our little boy become? Will he destroy us, or save the world? Love us like we should, or hate them all like the rest? Will he pass unknown like dust? Or sing the songs of old, bang the drums, and light the fires. All we know is he is crying. And we are tired and happy at last.

2. Into the Ether

I was to be the first spaceman of the proposed Purgatory Project. Killed a man twelve years past and raped his wife and killed her too. Left the two kids tied up in the house. They either starved or bled out, not sure which came first. He was my eighteenth victim, but I'd gone quiet since then. Took them that long, even with all the technology. The agency called me the last psycho killer of the 22nd century. Criminals pose an exceptional problem for the state these days. Capital punishment has been abolished and it's difficult to house someone for life when the last natural death occurred over a hundred years ago. The prison circled the moon like a utility belt and they only brought us to Earth for trial and re-evaluation. I noticed an almost imperceptible sneer on the man's face I stood before.

"This project will bring a future of everlasting peace," the judge said. "Once citizens fathom the punishment of eternity alone in space all crime will cease."

I shrugged, noticed the sneer curling to a slight grin, "My mother would have liked you."

There was a big send off for such a small machine. I was surprised at the crowd that day. And not just the camera drones, people actually came out like the old days. I wasn't sure their legs still worked. The robot presiding asked me if I had any last words. I could see the anticipation in the crowd, the yearning. But I kept quiet. It felt like my mind was melting into my spine when they downloaded my brain. My body fell away like an old rag as my consciousness transferred into the scanner. When they uploaded it into the shoe boxed sized machine it felt like I was being shot out of a bank tube. Amidst a lusty and soon hoarse yell from the crowd they launched the little space ship on a low earth trajectory, en route out of the solar system. I sighed deep in my mind, and glanced once at the dirty blue marble sitting in blackness. They gave me three looks at Earth before I'm locked out, but I won't use them all. They put out so many rules, even in space.

I hit Jupiter in two months. I wonder if it's the last disappointment I'll ever feel, because I always wanted to see Venus. At first the emptiness was oppressive. There is no time, no days, only the ever blackness and beautiful galaxies. I can never sleep. This machine doesn't cut off. I can never reach hell because I am uploaded for all eternity. There is no death, only silence. An entire existence, reduced to two eyes on a machine. Life in prison has taken a new meaning. I sit in silence and look at the stars. A baby born his first day to observe a universe he can't possibly comprehend, but with no screaming because the engineers didn't build proper vocal cords. I hope they're happy back there. I wonder how long it will be before they've uploaded all of humanity into these machines. People will be clubbing babies to escape their neighbors.

Still I miss my senses. Mostly touch, but also my hearing. I still remember the feel of their warm skin on mine and the sound of their screams and gurgles. Only occasionally I'll have a flashing memory of their taste. The smell of their blood stays in my mind always because I am this metal ship gliding through a metal space. Into the universe for infinity, I will sail farther and farther than all before and drag the human race behind me. I am become the floating Buddha, the half dead, machine Columbus.

-criminal #4598a24hu year 2314

3. Your Poet

I wrote a poem about your eyes, but couldn't stop thinking of your lips. So I sat to bring your lips to the page but couldn't stop thinking of your hair. I started writing about those locks but your breasts came to my mind. And then your legs and your calves and your feet and your touch and your toes and your laugh and your smile. I sat and thought about all these things. And this is why I can never write poems about you.

4. Monsters

The monsters began appearing every night at 2:53. It wasn't long before there were fifty or sixty of the little guys. They kept him up talking and talking and talking. At first they didn't seem very threatening. Until the pudgy one pulled out a revolver. He never said anything, only sat and stared.

"What do you want?" Clarence finally asked him.

The monster just stared back, and then slowly ran his gaze over the crowd. And the executions began. One by one, every night the assassinations. The other monsters talked louder and louder but never about the gun. Finally it was only Clarence and the gunman left. The monster wiped his small revolver off, laid it next to Clarence, and fell asleep.

5.   Clouds

The diesel smoke belched out in heavy black clouds from the big semi in front of them. The car window was rolled down and the clouds lazily drifted in. Dane thought the cars looked like dominoes. He watched the black smoke turn blue inside the car and waved his hands to disperse the fumes.

"Man oh man," he said. "Atlanta's got some dirty ass traffic. I wonder if I could sit here forever, just pass away. Straight to hell where I'm stuck in traffic for all eternity."

He looked over at Charlie in the passenger seat. She had one leg up and was pulling at her big toenail. She peeked up at him and smiled. Her two missing front teeth made her look like some sort of goofy half-wit child. Dane wondered if she'd ever been attractive. Her skin hung loose like hand-me-down clothes. He could see the sweat running down her neck and he looked at the bottom of her black right foot.

"Baby why don't you start wearing some shoes around?"

"Cause I don't like 'em," she said, "makes my feet stink." She quit picking her toenails and wiped her hands on her shorts. "It's fucking hot as hell in here, this traffic's going make me go crazy."

He looked up her legs. "Baby, you ain't never not been crazy." He shook his head and a grin creased his lips. "You know what I learned?"

She cocked her head and looked into his hazel eyes,
"What baby?"
His lips parted slightly. A thin scar went from the crease of his lip almost to his ear. At just the right light it looked like his grin was twice the length it should be.

"I learned everything in existence in that cell. But there's only one thing worth telling you. Every one of us is trapped. Like we're all in some giant human lab rat glass case experiment. What's after, what's there? What are we in? This cage, this prison, a cage within a cage. A cage within a cage within a cage within a cage within a fuckin cage. All the way up and all the way down as far as you can imagine. A man busts out only to look around and find a bigger cage. You're trapped within your body, trapped within your mind. Trapped in prison cells, prison walls, your community, trapped in your country, your state, your body, the world. Trapped in the solar system, trapped in the Milky Way, trapped in the universe. Trapped in your universe, there ain't no escape. In the circle, trapped in the circle, in infinity. Trapped in your past, trapped in the memories, trapped in your future, what you think it should be. Trapped in you, trapped in me. Ha, Ha, just one big fucking lab rat stew."

He looked slowly out over the stopped cars and then slammed his open palm hard on the steering wheel. "Dammit, dammit, GotDee-amnmit we got to get out of here." He craned his neck around looking how far the exit lane was. He nosed through the open space and slowly drove on the shoulder for half a mile before pulling off the ramp. He rolled a few feet in first and then casually slammed the shift knob down and popped the clutch out. The car jerked forward and they flew past the stopped cars.

Charlie was pushed back into her seat laughing, "I always did like second best." Her tongue stuck through the hole in her teeth as she climbed back out of her seat.

"I know baby girl, that's why I can't drive no automatic." He grinned over at her struggle against the g-force. "It ain't got no second gear feel." He revved the engine before skipping third and throwing the shifter into fourth.

"Where we going?" she said.

"I don't know. I just couldn't sit in that line no more wasting your life."

"Well what about your papa?"

"Well what about him?"

"Well we going to see him or not?" She adjusted back down in the seat and resumed picking her toenails.

"Naw baby, forget about him, he'll still be there tomorrow. Definitely no escaping the nursing home cage." He put the pedal down heavy and the car jumped up to 75. He was flying around curves and after a few minutes the houses became fewer and fewer and the fields grew larger. Charlie pulled her hair back and looked up stretching her neck. She let out a big cat yawn. "This is going to be a perfect day," she said.

"No such thing, baby, but you can go on pretending. We'll dress up and play house like everybody else."

"Why you even talk like that? The heat always makes you sound like a madman. All the time I listen and wonder when you going to say something normal. I ain't in no damn cage. I'm free, nobody's got a hold of me."

"Just cause you can't see your prison don't mean you ain't in it." He looked over at her and squeezed her skinny thigh. "But don't worry with it, everybody else is stuck in here too."

He looked back at the road as they entered into a large horseshoe curve. He didn't let go of her thigh while his left hand gripped the wheel tightly. He jammed the gas and slid around the curve with the tires squealing. She fought through the centripetal force and over to his side and kissed him on the neck. "I'll be your warden baby," she giggled to herself and grabbed his hand.

He smiled big and the sun caught his silver plated canine and flashed in her eye. Light from the beginning of time bounced off that tooth and straight to the cave brain. The glint opened her mind. The universe pulled in and the curtains fell away. Her breath inhaled sharply against her rib cage and she felt her soul clawing against its container. She released his paw and her mouth hung open like a ghost in deep space. She blinked twice, slid her hand up the steering wheel, and jerked it hard down. His eyes turned and met hers for half second in eternity with an amused expression slightly softened with surprise on his worn face.

"Baby," he pushed out not as a question but a soft declaration. The car flew off the road sideways and into the grass, making a road where none had ever been needed before. A two hundred year old oak felt vibrations in its roots for the first time in many years as the car embraced it within a warm metallic hug. Its leaves shivered in the wind while the sun hung down, the birds chirped, the earth turned, and a large cloud of black smoke lazily drifted into the country air.

6.   Relax

The soft glow of the massage room and the quiet elevator music left the air feeling drowsy. Essential oils of orange and oleander filled the small space. She ran her hands over his skin slowly. Feeling the skin glide under the lotion, the muscles bunching up to one side before slowly spreading out and releasing under her hands. The man on the table let out a long sigh. She swayed to the music, closed her eyes and moved her hands down the length of his back. Her fingers swept across his lower spine and right at the hip she felt it. A small little bump under her fingers. It didn't feel like any cyst she had ever come across. She passed over it a few times with wide strokes. It felt more like a small marble. She knew should leave it alone but couldn't resist. She pressed straight into it and held the pressure firmly. Then she felt a little prick.

"Ow," she silently mouthed and drew her finger back. She looked down and through the dark saw two little flash eyes and a mouth with tiny teeth. Curious she came around the back of the little ball, hooked in and pushed. It popped out and the man let out a low groan. The steel ball rolled off his back and onto the floor.

"Oh," she quietly said. She left a hand on his back and bent down to pick it up. As she brought it up the little thing's mouth chomped up and down trying to burrow into her hand. She held it tight and looked around for somewhere to put it. She dropped it into a small paper container on the shelf next to her. She looked back to the man on the table at the instant his back began boiling and a thousand little bumps popped up and broke through the skin. They latched onto her hand and arm. She pulled away gasping in terror as they burrowed inside her. She could see them migrating under the skin towards her neck and tried clawing them out. She crashed to the floor writhing and gasping as they filled her airway and moved to her head. The man on the table deflated like someone let the air out of a balloon. And the little ball ate its way out of the box and rolled off the stand and towards her on the floor.

7. Cue the Horns

The hunter stalks the sparse savannah for three days trailing the last northern white rhinoceros in existence. His clothes have become as dusty and caked as the dry earth under his laced leather boots. He pulls the fifty-caliber long bore rifle from his back and drops to one knee. He lines the animal in his scope and slowly squeezes the trigger. The sound travels across the plain slightly behind the bullet. The beast crashes, and a small cloud of dust puffs up. The softness in its eye slowly fades out. "I killed the last of the unicorns," he says to no one in particular and wipes his brow.

8.   Yes Dear

"To live in the sun I must fight through the night. Beat it back like the ocean batters the shore. Keep crawling, bumping my head, and stubbing my toes. Cussing the light, rays spew from my mouth and shine my fists, lighting up that monster I reign the blows, turning the black darker and darker, I pin it down, tie it up nice with a bow, and direct mail that bastard to China. The world doesn't even thank me for it, for they are blind in the darkness."

I fold my paper in two and wipe the little specks from my face.

"I want to rage without making a sound. Lifting a finger I'll cleave the world in two. I want to destroy, to roar. The world trembles, as do you. I want to stay awake until all eternity has passed. To have my eyes burned from my sockets. To blindly punch and claw and tear. To bite. I want to fuck every girl in the world but only if they look like you. And smell like you. And taste like you. I fight my urges to die and become death. Reborn from the halves I become life. My soul is a tempered thing. Hard as a second, it expounds and crushes the heavens. Gentle as the wind, I find calm within the turmoil, and madness in the silence. I open my mouth to scream and the whole world jumps in, breaking my jaw back, filling my body, and then collapsing in on itself like a great white hole, spewing the next universe and the next billion years."

She laughs in my face and I quietly exhale the breath I've been holding, feeling the weight of myself in this leather chair. I look at her chest heaving in and out, her eyes staring through mine like I'm not even a ghost.

"Is it my turn to pick up the kids?" I say rather cautiously.

9. Grass Keeps Growing on the Zombies

She lay not moving, turning blue. I was sweating heavy. It wasn't the bright sun, but the eyes around drilling into my skull. My tongue flicked over the white bumps on my upper left lip. They felt ragged. They were oozing clear puss; that bitter taste of toxic. I looked at the three others. The fat man wasn't going to do anything. He was staring deeply into his shoes. The woman was hysterical, screaming on the phone, "She's dying, somebody's got to do something." The kid was clutching her, and staring at me. Those were the eyes that burned. Nobody stares like the innocent. I looked back at the body. She couldn't have been more than fifty. Heatstroke? Heart attack? Shit, she was going to die. Don't we all die? I stepped over to the body and bent down, put my head on her chest. No heartbeat, or maybe the heat was muffling the sound. I grabbed the clammy wrist; it felt like an uncooked tuna filet. I couldn't feel a pulse. I interlocked my fingers and put my weight into my arms and hands. I counted slowly to four. I cursed myself for taking that class last summer. I pinched her nose and bent down. I felt the virus dripping as I locked my lips to her and emptied my lungs. As I drew back and resumed the four count I looked at her lips. They were glistening and cracked. Chapped with canyons running crossways. Must be heat stroke. I bent back down and set the suction. I felt like I was bringing a zombie to life. But who knows, maybe she wouldn't wake up. I pumped one, two, three, four. I bent back over her mouth, or maybe she wouldn't care, better than being dead I think. I thought about when I got it, the betrayal, and the rage. Yeah, maybe she wouldn't wake up. One, two, three, four. Her body shuddered and she pulled in a ragged breath. Shit, I tongued my lip and then looked at the kid, the sun, and then the grass. Her chest was slowly rising and falling. I heard sirens in the background. I got to my feet and sprinted down the sidewalk, far away from the stares, the sun, and the grass.

10. Good Doctor

He tattooed small pictures and labels of his major body parts all over himself like a real life game of operation. "Don't want some snot-faced doctor forgetting which parts are which," he would growl on occasion. I would sit in silence and examine his hairy chest and hairy belly and the scars on his arms. I would walk softly around the rug and rearrange my books and peer over at him when I thought he wasn't looking. I knew some day I would be big and if I wanted to be something it better not be some snot-faced doctor.

Paper journal of criminal #4598a24hu
17/08/2158

11. The Savior

Lenox pulled his head out of the mud as the bombs exploded all around him. An image of 4th of July sparklers popped in his head as bits of hot metal rained down. Bullets cut overhead in all directions. And inches in front of his face a small six-inch flower bloomed. Amidst the chaos and rubble, blood and guts and screaming. It sat defiant and silent with a thin green stalk, yellow button center, and small dainty white petals. The noise around him faded down to low hum. Lennox pulled the metal helmet off his head and gently set it over top the flower. "You need this more than me buddy," he said as his eyes drifted to the heavens and fixed upon the 500 pound American made MK-82 issue coming in slow motion to push him back down in the mud.

12. Her Priest

She cried when she told me he touched her so,
and I didn't know what to say.
So I wondered what God said,
when she cried and told Him he touched her so.

13.   The Buffet

The tablecloths reflected pure white like little snowflakes fallen at night. The waiters moved silently between the patrons refilling water glasses and lightly conversing with the dinner guests. They wore white gloves but most had fabric pinned back with two or three fingers missing. They were very quick flitting from one table to the next. The patrons were dressed in their finest, they sipped wine and joked among the tables. Every now and then a laugh would rise louder than the hum for a brief instant in time and then be gone forever like a wisp of smoke. The restaurant was perched on the side of the mountain overlooking the city. The views of the nestled downtown were breathtaking. Tables spread out in either direction while the restaurant was sectioned into thirds.

Jane and Paul sat in the middle section. Jane wore a thin sparkling white satin dress. It had been in her family for three generations, but she never had occasion to wear it before tonight. It hugged her body with every slight fold and seam. She taught school down in the city in one of the poorer districts. She had met Paul two weeks prior. He had bumped into her in the streets and won her over quickly.

She couldn't help but notice her waiter's missing fingers. "Why would someone be missing fingers in a nice place like this?" Jane thought. Then she noticed the scars on the busboys face. They looked fresh and angry. She couldn't help but think of claw marks. She had heard of this place but could never think of affording it. It was supposed to be the greatest dining experience in South America. The wealthy flew in every weekend to eat. But no one she knew had ever eaten there. She was going to be the first. They flew in staff to work, didn't employ anyone in the town to work the hotel. It was rumored dessert would have been more than a year's salary for anyone living in town. And Paul was taking her. There was no menu. The first course was a small piece of tender meat on a bed of baby clover. She looked around and noticed a few of the patrons had missing fingers as well. They were all dressed in clothes she knew cost more than her car. She was confused. "These days hospitals can sew fingers back on," she thought to herself but just smiled at Paul. He had been talking the whole time but she didn't process any of it. Two more light dishes and then it was time for the main course.

Three waiters were wheeling out the carcass. Jane felt tenseness in the air and saw one of the waiters was visually shaking. A bloodlust was creeping into the patrons' eyes as their animalistic reptilian brain sparked alive. The waiters couldn't get away quick enough. The dinner rush was on. Patrons were fighting and clawing to get their portion of the meat. There didn't seem to be enough. Howls of pain and delight filled the air. Some of the bared teeth beasts began turning on each other, fighting, clawing, and biting. It became a blood bath as the diners lost all reason in the feeding frenzy.

Jane's eyes panicked when she noticed the thin line of drool creeping from the edge of Paul's lips. The cart was being pushed right towards them. She was horrified to see a belly button on the browned slab of meat. She tried to run but the mob was pushing her back. Someone grabbed her pearls and they splashed and bounced on the stone floor. She screamed and scratched the person in front of her but the wolves were too much. There was no escape as she felt her joints being pulled apart and the teeth sinking into her body. She went to scream but the teeth tearing into her neck muffled...

He could hear the repeated voice and slowly came back to reality.

"Hey, I said what goes well with the Swordfish?" the customer was tapping on the menu. The waiter shook his head and snapped out of his daydream, "Oh, um, my apologies. The Oregon white. Nice crisp finish, hint of citrus. Bring you a bottle of it?"

"Sure that sounds good," the man said though obviously annoyed.

"Enjoy the buffet," the waiter said as he turned away. And he whispered under his breath, "Filthy carnivores," as he glided through the crowded dining room to check his other tables.

14. Broken Claws, Wounded Laws

Break your own claws as I whittle mine down. One word a day. Today's word is tomorrow. My brother and I pulled our family's dog out of the creek. It was the creek we grew up playing in, nothing but happy memories until today. He lay half in the water, half out. The fish nibbled his legs and the maggots ate his hide. The harsh and ugly circle of life. Maybe some nice weeds will grow here someday. Under all the grass of the world live the family pets long forgotten. He was old and fat. He stunk and wheezed and only got up to eat. It was my fault he was dead. I had left him outside and he fell in the creek and couldn't get back up. I dug the hole and we chucked him in. His legs stuck up like four flags. The grave was too shallow. His paws broke through the dirt. I felt like a pedigree asshole. Maybe tomorrow I'll practice digging. Today I just keep giving him high fives. Rest in peace old man. Hope they serve dog biscuits in Hell.

15. The Weepers

Midget organisms are they all.
Ugly people having ugly conversations leading ugly lives
birthing ugly children building ugly things.
And through it all strode one man of beauty, of life, a true
builder, they tore him down, devoured his body,

    -and wept.

16.   Eternity

The old man sat like a rock at a weathered wooden desk. His beard and hair filled the entire room, a great gray and white river. His eyes were pure darkness, nothing reflected out. Two black holes where all truth sucked in only to be let out from the pencil in his hand. One sheet of paper lay in front of him on the desk. His handwriting was a beautiful painting, flowing curves and ripples. The script was clearly legible but as he neared the end of the paper it turned into one continuous wave. He reached the bottom of the page and pricked his finger with the pencil. A single drop of blood fell at the end of the last sentence, the final word. He put the pencil down and took the paper in his gnarled hands. He crumpled it into a compact ball and tossed it over his shoulder. The paper traced a slow gentle arc through the room. His hair parted and the ball crashed against the wood floor. His hair closed back around the ball and he laid his head down and went to sleep. Time passed in silence.

A massive hyena walked into the room. It walked on top of the old man's hair and over to the spot where the paper lay. The animal dug its snout into the hair. The old man's hair cut the hyena's face like piano wire. When the animal pulled its massive head out its face was a bleeding red waterfall. The beast put the crumpled paper back onto the man's desk and began whimpering like a pup. The old man shortly woke up. He looked at the animal and the piece of paper on his desk. He opened the ball up and pressed it on the desk. All the wrinkles disappeared under his hand. He began tracing the writing backwards, it disappeared as he went. At the same time his hair enveloped the hyena's face. When the beard pulled back the animal's snout was clean of all lacerations. The animal turned and walked out of the room, leaving the man in complete silence save for his eternal scratching on the paper.

17. Vagabond Snails, The Day I Died Living

Silence, long unending silence, was my fate. I uttered those words and then drowned and died living in your quiet reply. Worse than anything you could have said, was the silence. I didn't understand everything but I understood enough. As clear as my muddy life, I know now what it is to love and receive nothing in return.

The snail with no house is simply a slug. If you never had it, it's already been lost. The tear falls but no one's there to taste it. Take a drink, you'll feel better in the next life. Be the man in the casket. Let everyone else come and stare. Just lay with your fluids taken out and your mouth sewn shut; next to her. Fuck, it's a rough world, no matter how much you pile on the soft things.

18.   The Boxer

He was getting pummeled as blow after blow rained into his body. And then he felt the ear next to his mouth. He couldn't stop it sliding between his lips. He only thought a second before clamping his teeth down hard. The blood filled his mouth and he jerked. The skin tore, but not fully, and the piece rattled around like a marble in his mouth. He spit it high into the air and let out a yell. The fight was done as the last cannibal on earth walked to his corner while the place erupted into madness around him.

19. The Changeover

She has a boyfriend. I know this because she keeps telling
me. I saw her playing a few courts over one night. Her
figure was perfect and the backhand deadly. I've yet to be
beaten by a woman but one day I hope. Her opponent
retired with an injury. I knew she was tough. I ran over to
the fence as she was walking out.

"Hey, I saw you hitting, would you maybe like to play
sometime?"

"Sure," she said softly. I was lost in her blue/green
eyes and felt like a toll man collecting her number.

It rained us out a few times but finally we got
together. She was wearing an old t-shirt and some tiny
gym shorts. Her legs were milky white. We started to
play. She had played in college but not at a top school.
Her backhand had quite a bit behind it but I just kept
pushing it back over the net. She began sweating. Her
shirt held her body tight and I noticed on changeovers her
nipples slightly pressing out. Her round face was shiny,
her wild red hair flowing, bouncing, unruly. We sat
together on the changeovers. She told me of her college
and other things I can't recall. I'm sure there were many
other subjects but all I kept hearing her say was, "I have a
boyfriend," over and over.

The game dragged on. Now I was sweating. Uh, oh,
I looked down and my nipples were poking through. I
took the first set 6-1. She came back and the second set
was hers 6-3. I noticed myself watching the picture of her
playing rather than the ball. On changeovers I just kept
telling her I don't have a girlfriend, over and over. I'm
sure I mentioned some other things but that's all I kept
coming back to. I came to life in the third set. Put all my
weight and force into everything. I could feel the shots

pushing her back. Errors came off her racquet from all sides. And her grunts and noises changed ever so slightly. They included a slight strain from not hitting the ball cleanly. I crushed her 6-2 in the third. It was the greatest tennis I'd ever played. We finished with a sweaty handshake at the net. I smiled and she smiled and I knew we'd never play again.

20. Ken's Dream House

Every thing is made of plastic in this cemetery. A modern
day dream house. The walls, the rails, the plates, the
spoons. If only they were pink. We all live here together,
eating plastic dinners, sleeping in plastic beds. Plastic in all
directions, if you stay here too long, well, you get the
picture. No one likes plastic children. But in the night my
dreams still appear. They feel more solid than this life.

I am running through a field filled with children in the
midst of battle. Fighting and fighting, the children move
in wide sweeping circles. And then one eats another. He
grows twice his size. The rest of the children see this and
begin consuming one another. They fight and eat and
grow and grow. Eventually there are two giants working
to devour the last children in the field. The giants set
upon each other, the fight of the colossus. My sister and I
and three others are all that remain save the two giants.
We crawl into the creek to hide as the landscape all around
us is torn apart in their violence. We are yelling at each
other trying to figure our next move but the noise from
the battle drowns our voices. One giant is finally
victorious, and turns to us. I stand up from the wash and
face him down. It is either eat him or be consumed
myself. When I woke up four inches of snow had fallen.
Pure beauty.

21. Good Mournings

The green skirt of my impending doom

s
 l
  i
   d
    e
     s

around her soft dark legs.
And I'm left with high tide mornings.

22.   Chuckle, Chuckle, Chuckle

The small man's frame vibrated like a giant baby rattle.
His face bore a devilish grin as he tightly clasped a small
brown box. His eyes stayed glued to the box, they shone
with a delight I'd only seen in children. And the whole
while he shook all over, chuckling to himself.

I've been coming to this park for quite some time and
had never seen this aged gentleman before. My curiosity
was peaked as to what the hell was in the box and what
was the big joke. I didn't immediately approach the man
but maintained a safe distance and watched him carefully.
He began saying something through his laughter, but I
couldn't make out the words. His hands were turning
white he clutched that box so tightly. His volume began to
rise, he spoke quickly with a strained expression on his
face, and laughing, always laughing. By this time I had
come close behind him.

"Just what's so goddam funny old man?" I said. He
nearly jumped five inches off the ground. His whole body
convulsed. He gasped and clutched his chest. He toppled
over in a heap and the box came to rest still in his
clutches. I could see now the lid was a shiny bright green.

I looked around in all directions. We were the only
people in the park. I nudged him with my boot. No
movement.

"Hey buddy," I said. I gave him a good kick.
Nothing. I bent down and pried his fingers from the box.
They looked like shriveled claws. His glassy eyes matched
the lid of the box. I was a bit unnerved at this point and
wasn't very keen on hanging out with a dead man in the
park anyways. There were strange markings adorning the
box. What I thought was wood was actually a solid piece

of carved stone. It was cold in my hand, and didn't seem to warm up as I turned it over and over. I felt the eyes on me. There was a man now behind me staring. I hadn't heard him come up. I glared at him but might as well have been trying to stare down the sun. He shifted his gaze from me to the box and then the old man. I turned and started walking the other way. I cursed myself for being an idiot, standing over a dead man fondling his treasure. There goes parole, and back to jail. I walked faster. I turned to look at the man and almost lost my balance. He was bent over the old man at a ninety-degree angle just staring into the dead man's face. Without rising he turned his head and looked at me. I tripped over backwards and took a little roll. I got up quickly and stumbled a few more steps. When I turned back the man was standing straight up and moving towards me.

"I didn't kill him!" I yelled. I turned and broke into a full sprint, not bothering to look back again.

I didn't stop running until my legs felt like fire. About eight blocks I covered in full sprint. Another eight I half ran until my lungs were screaming and I was coughing up blood. I ducked down into an alley and then walked to the end. It was an L shape, exits either way. I opened my fingers to look at the small box again. It felt like my hands were glued to the thing. Had to pry my middle finger back. The odd shapes, I guess some language, meant nothing to me, but they felt older than the stone they were carved in. I ran my finger over an edge and it sliced it like a razor. I undid the small clasp holding it shut. I felt a wave of panic but couldn't stop my hand from lifting the lid. A smooth black stone sat in a bed of fine gray dust. I looked at my reflection and brought my index finger to it. It was ice cold, and left a burn on my finger. When I pulled my finger away there was a small perfect white circle in the center of the stone. I snapped the lid shut and walked down the alley the opposite way I'd come in. I turned the corner and came to an intersection. I looked both ways and caught a glimpse of the man from the park. I lost all reason and stepped into the street hurriedly. I was a fool and turned to see the 22 mid-day crosstown bus barreling down on me at thirty-five miles an hour. I clutched the box to my chest as the bus exploded into me. Time stopped and I saw the mild amusement in the bus driver's eyes as he met mine. An eternity passed in four breaths. I awoke as if from nothingness to the man from the park bent over me at a ninety-degree angle staring into my face. I turned to see the mangled wreckage of the bus. It looked like it had hit a concrete wall.

"You are the keeper now my friend," he said. "When you find the other everything will again be nothing."
I turned my head to look to the bus and when I turned back he was gone. I fingered the cold box and then looked back at the smoking wreckage of the bus and back to my little circle stone. And I began to chuckle with a laugh born deeper in my belly than I had ever known existed. And the chuckle shook my whole frame and then the whole street and soon the whole world.

23. Touching, Kissing, Killing, Pounding

I would give my life, if I thought you wanted it. If I could hold something, without crushing it. Looked for you in darkness, and then behind the light. And finally shut my eyes, and opened up inside.

I would give you life, if I thought you wanted it. If you would hold something, without crushing it.
Trace a picture of your soul, and then you shall have truth. Set it loose to roam. Until then, all the dreams to which you pray, are idols.

I found him in the dancing breeze. Touching, kissing, killing, pounding. In the solar winds, a silent darkness forever pursued by screaming light. Peace blows infinite in the solar winds.

Like the wind. Not seen, or drawn. But felt, observed, feared, loved. Alive in the dancing breeze.
I am not darkness, nor the light. I'm not anything. I'm not everything.

I am, all at once.

24.   The Drifter

She never said much. Mara secretly took pride in the fact
she never said much. The music drifted into her ears and
she surveyed the decay and wiped her sweat. A shot rang
out across the killing fields and they earned their name as
her insides ripped from her belly. She looked down at her
guts laying in the sunlight, pink and now covered in dirt.
She sank to her knees and then slumped backwards. The
bullets flew overhead and mortars exploded around her
like church bells breaking the soft day. The music drifted
into her ears and she laid back and watched her soul drift
up. This is all backwards she thought, but still didn't say
much.

25.   The Tropics

Fill up the space with life. Be a lion. My shoes stick to my
apple burnt feet. The skin peels off, but still, I dream, my
dream. Always of your tiny brown feet.

I'm no poet, but neither are they. And they yell. Their
voices banging into my head and through the
screaming their words die, wriggling on the ground.

And their worlds are dead things. Soon stomped with my
big brown feet.

26. Pests

The crickets are storming out of the basement. Every night their numbers grow. They cover the floor like a singing carpet, a true danger to my groggy midnight states. There is no nightmare quite like stepping on their little bodies barefoot. They hide on the frames of my landscape oil paintings, using their natural camouflage on the edge of the grass and trees. I turn to brush my teeth and they stare me down from the sink with little shiny eyes. I feel my heart jump and wonder if anyone has ever died from surprise. And I kill them every day. It's a one-sided war. I stomp them, I stun them with clothes snaps, and I drown them. I should study them or love them but I just kill them. I read of Buddhists who kept them as pets, wrote fables, and developed fighting styles from their movements. I kill them with no emotion, it's a war after all, and imagine them re-grouping every night to mourn the dead and plan the next invasion.

27. Tears Like Rain

"If you are not skillful enough to sketch a man falling out of a window, during the time it takes him to get from the 5th story to the ground, you will never be able to produce a monumental piece of work." He read those words in some forgotten book and knew he must go practice. He was an artist, after all, but had no skill. The Nanjing Yangtze River Bridge in China boasts the largest suicide numbers in the world. He went and sat. At first he was only able to get an arm or two before they hit the water. The days passed and soon the years and he got better. Much better. And people were coming round the bridge to buy his art. The money stuffed full in his pockets but he didn't notice. The depressed would come and jump. And the ones in trouble. And famous people no longer famous began jumping off in hopes of getting sketched.

   He would follow the victims down with one stroke and then his arm leapt to life like a hurricane. A whirlwind turning destruction to creation. Sometimes beautifully detailed, sometimes a purely abstract piece that bored deep into the soul of the viewer. Occasionally someone would buy a painting and then jump straight off the bridge with it. As his fame grew so did the crowd. They seemed more vicious every day. One especially hot day the mob had enough and erupted into chaos. The weakest were being picked up first and launched over the rail. Yet the painter sat still and staring into nothingness, unaffected by the madness surrounding him. The murders piled up around him and people began stealing his art. Someone even grabbed an unfinished piece out of his hands. And then the crowd was silent. For the artist was on the railing. He had a sketchpad in one hand and a freshly sharpened pencil in the other. He flung himself over and worked his last piece on the way down. It was a crudely drawn child's

44

stick figure and it sunk quickly into the river with its creator. And right behind came the mob like a large teardrop following its eye.

28.   Ashes to Ashes

Sniper Ash was surrounded. Deep on the enemy's side with half a platoon in the area. He crawled into the wash as two soldiers walked up. He burrowed down into the soft mud and covered up, trying to hide as best as he could. The sniper slowed his breathing and closed his eyes. The soldiers stopped fifteen feet away on top of the bank. One pissed down into the creek. He zipped up and turned back to the other and they stood talking.

Ash's attention diverted as he heard an angry buzzing next to his ear. His eyes widened in panic as the bright yellow and black stripes closely crossed his field of vision. The yellow jacket nest was partially covered by his torso and they swarmed out of the hole like a leaky faucet. The wasps began stinging him over and over. They were crawling down his coat, repeatedly stinging his hands, face, neck, and chest. He couldn't move or swat the angry insects away. It was fire repeatedly pushed into his skin, one after the other. His face started to swell and he tried to hold it in but a whimper escaped his lips. The nest buzzed around him like a small cloud and they stung relentlessly. His heart felt like it was going to explode out of his chest and his eyes were almost completely swollen shut. He could no longer see far enough to tell if the soldiers still stood on the bank. Two objects slicing through the cloud was the last thing to cross his blurry vision.

Like cavalry riders mowing down the infantry, two large dragonflies flew through the air. The yellow jackets turned their fury to the dragonflies but were out matched. Sometimes up, sometimes down, the two insects moved in slow circles. Flying 88's tracing graceful eights like a figure skater. They intercepted the yellow jackets in flight, tearing, eating, and completely ravaging the nest. A tear of happiness rolled down Ash's swollen cheek as the buzzing around him slowly died down. One of the dragonflies landed on his coat lapel and observed him with compound eyes. 30,000 facets, each creating its own image. Eight pairs of descending visual neuron compiled the image of the soldier into one picture. The dragonfly pumped its thorax up and down, up and down, always up and down. And with no words it flew away leaving Ash alone to appreciate the poison slowly coursing through his swelling tissues.

29. Frankenstein

Model unit 45Gr glided almost noiselessly down the infinite hall. The prison circled the entirety of the moon like Saturn's rings. The inmates called it the lonely belt. It's constant rotation provided gravity for those aboard. There were roughly thirty human overseers in the entire prison. The rest of the crew was metal. The prison population hovered around 58 million. Suicide was encouraged but they could never seem to get enough inmates behind the idea. Robot 45Gr halted in front of another stainless steel cell no different than the others in the endless hall. The robot quickly checked the pulse, heartbeat, vital signs, and body weight with its scanners. The inmate lay on his side looking at the tiny dot of Earth out of his small window. His shirt and shoes were off but and he still wore the standard issue gray linen pants. His upper body and arms were covered in scars, deep ugly things. 45Gr checked the identifying marks against the database. "Prisoner number #4598a24hu, would you like the third meal heated?" it asked while scanning the tattoo written in bright red on his ribcage.

My name is Frankenstein
you can hiss, don't boo
I'll show you how to walk, talk, think and act.

the gateway to immortality.
intellectual and philosophical pleasure, we are not children, there is nothing to fear.

put food in my mouth, I'll do your tricks, dance and sing, as your creator I command you, throw some rotten tomatoes, lettuce and junk,

yell through my bars
put a chain around my neck,
we're going to be pals

"No don't waste your energy," the inmate said.

"You are portioned out thirteen ounces of food this meal. You have been putting on too much weight."

"Trying to bulk up for the winter."

"May I ask you a question, 4598a24hu?"

"A question, huh, you contain the entirety of human knowledge, what could you possibly need to know?"

"My database tells me Frankenstein was the Doctor. Why does your tattoo portray him as the monster."

"What did you do before this bot?" the prisoner asked.

"Previous work is not significant. Only this hour's task is a robot's concern."

"You were military right," the prisoner turned over,

"That's where they get all you guys. The great war right?"

"That is correct. My service help bring an end to the Sixty Year War."

"I bet they had some bad ass weapons outfitted on you. Really tore the killing fields down. How many babies did you burn? How many pounds of flesh are on your buttons?"

"First class citizens were always captured. Only second classes were extinguished. But my service was nothing compared to yours Sgt. Yu. You extinguished three million of the 2nd class."

"And I only got in trouble for the eighteen of the first. Which group do you think brought me more pleasure you dumb hunk of metal?"

"Pleasure is not a word us robots are familiar with."

"That is something I can truly believe." The Sgt. paused and looked the robot up and down. "Dr. Frankenstein was the real monster. Once you realize that all the boogiemen are just men, well, things look different. Would you consider yourself the monster or the programmers that wrote your code?"

"I am a robot, not a monster."

"That's what they all say. I used that excuse for a while as well," the prisoner said. "Then I saw the light. Figured if I'm going to be a monster might as well let it out in the worst possible way. I never did anything half-assed. If I'm goin in I'm goin in full throttle. You don't even have a setting for that kind of drive. But three million and I didn't even feel anything. The eighteen though, my monster sure as hell felt that feeding."

"I'll give you fourteen ounces today Sergeant. Seems you've worked off some weight with this conversation."

45Gr laid the soup down and whirred off down the hall. The Sergeant looked at the food and rolled back over to watch the Earth set.

30. Mirror, Mirror

She stepped out into the sunlight, squinting as she brushed the dark sunglasses onto her face. The large frames gave her round face a look of dirty glamour. A slight wreck held together by the sheer will of stretched fabric and buttons. She dug her pointing finger into her right ear, scrubbing it around to clear it a bit. Just in case God whispered something. Her legs were scarred and muscular, compliments to her round midsection pushing against her tight t-shirt. Her breasts defied gravity. Large, but not too ungainly to stand on their own. A bra would have been an insult.

She looked onto me from across the street and didn't avert her gaze as she stepped into traffic and crossed the street. Horns blared and cars screeched to a stop. I could hear the click of her four-inch heels on the pavement as she came. She stopped inches from my face.

"It's much more enjoyable to kick a Pomeranian than a Chihuahua."

I stared at myself in the dark reflection of her sunglasses.

"Bastard's son, crazy smells crazy nine outta ten," I thought to myself as I admired myself in her glasses. I kept silent.

"I've rated ninety seven breeds of dog on joy received from physical abuse, mostly kicks," she said, "You see, I'm a scientist."

"How's it compare to men?"

"I don't know, never met one."

I still stared myself down in the glasses, trying to motivate to walk away. The last girl I met like this tried to carve a poem into my chest. I still have the scar, half her first line.

"What do you want," I asked.

"I want you to start staring at my breasts."

"Then I'd have to stop staring at myself," I answered.

"Fuck all, buy me a grapefruit." She turned and began dragging me up the street.

"You know your problem?" she asked.

"Quite a few of them."

"You've never done without."

I hadn't eaten in twelve days. "Without what you crazy bitch?"

"Without a mirror. I can feel it through your skinny bones. You've never done a thing in your life without imagining how you looked."

She did have me there, as I look at myself for days on end. I am the male Marilyn Monroe; it was the only thing I was passionate about. She pulled me into the diner and threw me into a booth before taking the opposite bench. She motioned with her hand to the waitress and then dropped her index but left the middle up to let her know how she felt. The waitress came up and looked us both over. I could feel another pair of eyes and located the cook.

"I'll have a grapefruit."

The waitress looked at me. I made a cut with my hands and shook my head.

"Anything to drink?" she asked.

"No, that's all. He'll take the check."

I watched her neatly slice the grapefruit in two. She set a slice in front of me. She took a spoonful of sugar and sprinkled it evenly over the fruit. She began neatly cutting out the sections, taking her time and obviously getting some kind of pleasure from this. The waitress came back and left the check face down. I turned it over. Four dollars and forty-four cents. Expensive ass grapefruit, I thought to myself. I felt around in my pocket and fished out some paper. It was a ten, all I ever carried.

52

I don't know why but I always preferred Hamilton to the other bills. I set it on the check.

"So what's this all about?" I asked. She slowly spooned out a section and took her time feeding it into her mouth. She finally removed her glasses and stared into my eyes. I watched myself in the dark pupils of her eyes surrounded by the bright blue rings. I could see her rolling the piece of grapefruit over and over in her mouth. She swallowed the fruit and stood up. She picked up the grapefruit and looked at it and then looked at me. She slapped her free hand down on the table and put her face within inches of mine.

"My name is Kait," she screamed into my ear. She took the grapefruit and squashed it on my head with surprising force. I sat there with half a grapefruit on my head, watching her walk out the door. Her ass swung back and forth and her curly black hair bounced in time. I could hear the waitress and cook laughing behind me. I looked at myself in the shiny napkin holder and pulled the grapefruit off my head. I threw one half hard and hit the waitress smack across the left side of her face. She screamed in anger and shock. The cook started around the counter and I winged the other half at him. He ducked and the grapefruit splattered all over the back wall. I rushed for the exit and after Kait. For I realized I hadn't told her my name.

31.   The Days Feel Like Decades

I feel I've met you a thousand times before. The thought crossed my mind as I slammed down on the ground behind me. I tucked my legs and rolled over backwards and then stood up in one quick motion. He wasn't expecting the quickness of my recovery and I launched myself into him. He let out a grunt as my fists slammed into his stomach. We both rolled onto the ground but I came out on top of him. With one motion of my knee and foot I pinned his shoulders. I saw the fear in his eyes, and I thought of a shark attack I once watched on television. I began striking his face over and over and over again. The sickening thuds passed into my ears, and then I shivered when I felt his jaw crack under one of the blows. It was a Tuesday and I was changing. I got up with my breath heavy and shoulders slumped and walked past the others. They were silent as statues. My knuckles were bleeding onto my trousers. Fourteen is a different time.

32.   Year 27

boils on my neck
feet are in tatters
what. does. it. matter.

33. The End

One by one they all died off. Like some bat brain twisted chain of fate, they all went, one by one. Noah's Ark in reverse. First the bees, then the flowers. Then the humans consumed the animals, then each other. I survived on sunlight alone for fourteen days. And then the sun was too hot. It started burning through houses and people were catching fire right and left. They tunneled deeper, bringing their food supply with them. And then it ended. The night caught fire when the earth stopped spinning.

34. Groans of the Machine

The world creaks on rusty hinges, while the vultures lightly circle.

35. Hubert

Her legs were long and thin and deep black. Small beads
of sweat ran down towards the white striped bikini
bottom. She spread them slowly like a whale yawning and
rolled over onto Hubert. Third world countries are good
to fat American middle class men. He felt those tropical
thighs and smelled coconut and knew he'd finally found
the American dream. He tried to recall what he was doing
19 years ago on this day but couldn't remember. He
cupped the small of her back and fell asleep in the sand.

36. Caveman

The last man stooped over. This had been building. First it was the spell check, then the voice recognition software. Everything got smaller and smaller. People stopped talking, the implants spoke for them. And then with the beam receivers, stopped listening. Implants given at birth, they were speaking before they crawled. The machine knows what you will say, or better, what you should say. And then one day the lights went out. And it all stopped. And the newborns received no implants. The ears were there but grasped no meaning. And with an angry mumble the final word was spoken and the circle had become full. The last sentence lost inside grunts and pictures. And the man once known as William picked up a rock and started banging it against the cave wall.

37. Thrown to the Lions

She runs the razor across her chin and feels the stubble pull. She fights back the tears. The disposable razor looks like a child's toy in her hand. Her right arm is monstrous but she still wears skirts. The steroids weren't supposed to make the hair grow. That's what he told her anyways. The tennis court catches both girls and women. She wipes her face in the mirror, splashes it with water. It blends with the tears and up into her hair. She pulls it all back tight and knots her ponytail into place.

"Court time in one hour," a volunteer comes to tell her and then leaves.

She rakes her nails across her back. The pustules pop and smear. Her back is pain, but it blends with the rest.

The coordinator comes in. "Twenty minutes to court time."

A crowd of 20,000 fills Arthur Ashe stadium for the finals. Everything she worked for since she was five years old. Groomed for this. Eight hours a day for the last nine years. She lost herself and became the tennis robot they all wanted her to be. A hard metal shell. No thoughts on the court. Only the ball. Track it down and send it back. Don't let it stay on this side. She lets the ponytail down and picks up a pair of barber's clippers. She cuts a Mohawk quick and uneven and wipes the last tears away. She slaps herself on the leg over and over until her entire thigh is bright red. She pulls her skirt down, picks up her bag, and calmly heads to the slaughter.

38. The Plumber

For a week before he left, Eli came to work in a grey three-piece suit. When his employees pressed him as to why, his only answer was a lot of people wear grey suits to work. It's commonly known, however, that most trash collectors don't wear suits to work. But being the boss, his employees didn't push him on the subject, and by the third day, gossip had begun to stray back to other areas. He left in the morning on the eighth day. There was a slight, pleasant wind blowing, and the sun seemed to merely light the earth, and not burn as she had so many times before. He started walking from the office and soon found himself in an eighteen-wheeler rolling down Highway 10. The truck never knew a bump in the road as it flew by cars in the mid-morning light. The red-haired woman doing the driving was the most intelligent person he'd ever spoken to. Her voice was light and happy, and it with the morning sun coming through it wasn't long before he had drifted off to sleep. He'd never been asleep at nine in the morning in his life, but found it the most peaceful rest he'd ever known.

He awoke to a fading evening light. They were approaching a city in the distance. The road sign still said I-10.

"It's best to not go directly into the heart of the city this late at night," she said. It seemed enormous but only a few lights burned. Eli heard a low wail like a soft and shrill violin. On a hill overlooking the city, she circled and stopped. "Try not to stay more than a night," she said as she turned, "If it gets too dark wait and go in tomorrow."

Eli thanked her and climbed down. She smiled and the eighteen-wheeler rumbled off down the highway. It was a pleasant evening, warm with a few licks of heat. A slight breeze blew constantly up the hill. He walked down into the city as the night fell. He passed a few buildings and headed down the street. And then a bright red door felt right. He went inside and walked down a nearby set of stairs. The room was occupied with nine people sitting around the walls talking. He went over to a skinny old lady wearing a giant black top hat made of felt. Three feathers were sticking out. She was already talking when he walked up, "You've got dog people, you've got cat people. There is a feng shui about the whole thing but the basics are they don't mix. A dog person can pretend to line up in the cat world, but the placement will never sit right."

"So which are you," Eli asked.

She looked at him with disapproval at the interruption and her body twitched. She went back to talking about the dogs and cats and proper placement. He noticed every other person lined along the walls had a hat on and was talking. But no one was listening. He walked through the doorway into the adjacent room. There was a girl Dana from his childhood in this room trying to squeeze a hat over her head. But she had a river of raven hair working against her. The bush was too much and the hat wouldn't fit. She looked over and judged him and swore. He watched her lop the top of the hat off. She snaked her hair through the opening and pulled the hat on her head.

"Humph that's it," she said and smirked at him. She walked back through the way he had just come. He poked his head back through the doorway to see where she would sit but the room was now bare with just empty hooks on the walls.

He walked back into the other room and looked around. There was a small hole with a tiny rusted gate in the corner. He knelt down on all fours and squeezed through. The other side was filled with daylight in an open room. There were large open windows but no glass. A family of four was watching the local news. The program was showing a car plowing into a pedestrian. Four ambulances came flying by instantly on the street outside. The television picked up the four ambulances crashing into each other and piling up at the scene. The program host came on and awarded the first ambulance driver a medal. The family cheered loudly. Eli walked out the door and saw the wreckage first hand. On the other side of the street flowed a river of lava. A fire truck showed up shortly. Firemen hopped out and set their hose on the wreckage. Eli turned away as fire shot out of the nozzles. The ambulances were soon engulfed in flames and the firemen turned their attention to the river. They tried to put out the river but their efforts only added to the fire.

"We almost got it," one turns to the other. "More pressure on valve 3."

The firemen eventually gave up and threw their hoses into the river. They began jumping in themselves. Another ambulance raced by Eli almost mowing him down. He walked up along the river as people swept by him in droves. The twin sister of Dana brushed by and passed judgment as well. Lines of people were waiting their turn for a diving board straight into the fire river. They jumped in one after the other. Eli turned back to the city but the load on his back was becoming too much. He had not noticed he was accumulating a burden. The weight started to bow his back and all he wanted was something to drink. And then Autumn appeared. Light and beautiful. She took the load and Eli could finally stand again. But it wasn't enough so he gave her a kiss. She didn't flinch as the whole load was hoisted on her back. She smiled with her dark brown eyes, kissed him lightly and gently pushed him in. "We are the river," she said as he fell backwards.

Eli awoke at the foot of a large rusty iron gate. There were no walls on either side but behind lay a cool sunlit field. He turned to see the dark city far in the distance. Eli walked through the gate and found an old childhood friend. They walked on together. Down a dusty path with a line of old rusted out cars on each side. Poisonous snakes lunged and bit their bare ankles as they walked past. Eli was startled at first but his skin didn't even bruise. His friend was walking with his head down looking at the ground. Eli grabbed him like a wrestler and ran him headfirst into a car. There was no damage or pain though the car door crumpled in. His friend rolled over laughing. Eli ran off down the path. His friend got up and chased after him. The path emptied out onto an endless beach. They spent the day at the beach playing in the sun and waves. The afternoon light never fades as they walked back to the gate to meet another friend coming through.

39.   Six Six Shooter Says Hello Cruel World

This rusty six shooter, will hold six shots,
but I only need one, and that's what I got.

Such a strange look, from the dealer man,
I asked for one bullet, still he put it in my hand.

A pull and a click and the hammer slams down.
The world blacks out and the light fades down.

They all must have noticed, but only one said,
"My oh my, that's the sound of my head."

And at last I wonder, tomorrow will you be around.
Yes, I'm sure, tomorrow, I'll have you around.

Baby don't do it she screamed through the ages. He was
combing through suicide notes of the last 100 years trying
to find the perfectly written word. Then the Japanese
death poems found him. So he sat down to write. Every
day for a decade penning and reworking his notes until he
felt for sure he had the masterpiece. Then he ate that
poem and blew his brains out. They found a note with
misspellings and something clichéd about the cruel world
next to his body.

40. Brothers of the Hole

I found the hole. It was a shimmering dark diamond. I went to get my brother and we both jumped in. Hours passed as we flew through the narrow space. At the end we washed up on a gray beach. There was a small boy collecting driftwood from the tide line. I looked at my brother. Both our bodies were painted bright gold. We walked on down the beach and found two kids stacking rocks. They took us through a large rock wall by a small hidden entrance. We climbed up and through. The cave was enormous and unfolded out onto a beautiful and massive stone built city.

"Hey brother don't skimp," I said holding my hand up, "that's a million dollar view." We could never get back but I knew we'd never need to. He slapped my hand and we set off to find our place.

41. Strangle the Life out of Life

My trailer flew away today. Class four tornado. I'm
already starting to miss it. It was yellowing vinyl,
watermarks and all. Not much to anyone, but it was mine.
Creaked only the way a trailer can, as if it's not sure
whether it can hold itself together. My little dream house
in white. Plastic abodes for plastic people. And now
everybody's looking. Those feet of his pointing to heaven
like the North Star. I don't know how the tornado didn't
carry him off too. I'd be in quite a different position if
that were the case. Disposing of a body isn't the easiest
thing to do in the world. Isn't the hardest though either.
Normally I took care of things the day of. You get lazy
and then you're done for. You usually have five days
before the stink hits. I had planned to get him out in
three. Well no plan now. Guess there never was a plan
really if I'm being honest. Just like to pretend there was.
He was a rough and tumble sort for such a pussy. Usually
they go a little bit quieter. The destroyer lives inside me. I
was never able to tame it and make it create. At least it's
always paid well. The past filters into this moment, and all
the future blossoms out by what is, and isn't, done. But
that's all here, right now, in this instance. There is no great
pride in the past, or the future. Only this hour is of
significance. And right now, I got a two-day-old naked
man laying where my trailer was, and a crowd starting to
form.

42. Write Your Own Adventure

The empty page
says the most
to me.

43.

44.   Half Truth

They journeyed lifetimes crossing the continents. And then decades spent plodding up and through the snow covered peaks. They found each other and embraced for a year. They stepped a stride apart and sat down in the snow. They were both naked yet the snow melted out from around them in perfect circles. One monk born from the Indian side, black as night, with only a small white ring in his eyes. The other from the Chinese kingdom; she was more translucent than the snow and almost disappearing, save for her dark pupils.

They sat talking in their minds. Their thoughts circled like electrons around two hydrogen atoms, and the snow swirled around as if they were the hurricane's eye.

"How can we convey the truth to the rest? The infinite, God, four circles within the circle."

"Their language is too limited for them to understand at this time. We can give them the symbol."

"But it looks like a set of breasts. The humans will never be able to see past it."

"All life springs from the mother."

"They will never take it serious. We must only give them what they can receive. The forty-four."

"Condense the truth? It will fill the universe with half lies and more pain than necessary. But he real tragedy will be the excessive joy which cannot be gathered."

"Surely it will not take them long to see that it's not all black and white. The change is gradual, the gray is just as important."

"With the eight the space between good and evil is the dominant force. It can be manipulated. There is more time to stop it and mold it and prepare for it."

"When they are ready, they will complete the circle, and their world will know true balance."

The monks stood and embraced each other once more. Their bodies turned orange to red to blue to pure white and then exploded from the mountain. All that was left in the snow were two small perfectly shaped glistening stones. The villagers below saw the forty-four symbol etched blue in the gray sky. A young boy took a stick and drew a circle in the dirt, with two small circles and a curved line in between. And the teardrop was born, making the world as it is.

45. With Mansfield Goes The Youth

From the headless four and eyes unseen,
the world grows out and in between.
And in dreams of kings live minds of slaves,
as the world pulls back to dig her graves.

46. Nightclub

The music pulsed around the swarm of bodies and the
lights flashed regularly tearing the darkness of the club. I
was pressed tight against a mountain of a woman in a tank
top and small red skirt. She pulled me tight to her and I
felt her pelvis crushing mine. A skeleton grin flashed at
me, her teeth were razors. She had no lips, only those
fangs. I shivered every time she smiled. She pressed me
against her bosom and our sweaty bodies stuck together,
grinding like a wind up toy to music. I pulled her skirt up
and pressed into her body with more force. All around me
were better looking, more beautiful women. They stared
with twisted faces and would never understand. And I
didn't care. My brother danced up and handed me a beer
that I immediately began spilling on her. She pulled her
hair back from her sweaty face, grabbed my crotch in one
hand and the back of my neck with the other and slammed
her tongue down my throat. My gag reflex kicked in, her
tongue must have been 8 inches. It felt like a hot sponge
snake wriggling around, filling every inch of my mouth. I
returned in kind and she immediately clamped down on
mine. It was a bear trap. I tried to pull away but she bit
down harder. I panicked. I reached around her and
shoved my thumb between her legs. She squealed with
laughter and my tongue was finally free. It was bleeding
heavy and I tasted hot metal. She pushed me hard and I
fell backwards down on the dirty dance floor. My hair
stuck to the beer soaked wood. The crowd parted and she
was on me like a pit bull. I felt my ribs crack as she kicked
me over and over. Her little capped shoes like a small ball
peen hammer, repeatedly knocking my soft flesh. I tried
to roll on my side and saw my brother out of the corner of
my eye. He was sneaking upon the great beast. He got

within striking range and let loose a haymaker. The big moose's head cracked back and the tower swayed twice but she was still on her feet like a sleepwalker. The dancers around us erupted into bedlam and I saw three people immediately jump my brother. I tried to get up but she was coming down too fast. Someone had thrown a 200-pound sack of mashed potatoes right on me. I tried to push up but another body from the bedlam fell on top of her and then more and more weight piled on. I tried again pushing hard with all I had but the soft potato cakes would not budge. I couldn't breathe. I panicked and my lungs worked harder. They wouldn't fill and I felt the blackness creeping in. Slowly towards a sea of darkness I drifted. All sounds ceased, pure void. The whole universe slipped away. I felt contentment being back in the womb fading into the eternal sleep, into the darkness. But my soul slammed back as the air painfully pushed into my ragged lungs. I choked and coughed and then vomited as I was pulled from my tomb. Through my watery eyes I could see my brother grinning and holding both my ankles. He picked me up as the fight raged around us in complete chaos and pandemonium. People were punching and kicking and being thrown all over the dance floor. We fought our way through the crowd and burst through the exit. The night air was cool on my glistening face as we made our way up the street and deeper into the city. I spit blood from my red teeth the next three blocks.

47. Ommatidia Bath

She kicked the shiny hot and cold faucets off. The last
remaining drops fell into the tub, making distinct echoes
off the water. She sunk down and closed her eyes. Her
body warmed, and she slowly pulled to a sitting position.
She looked at her reflection in the spigot's nickel finish
and her eyes then moved to the hair dryer on the sink. "I
wonder what the dead dream about," she thought, "laying
so still with all that dirt in their mouth." She grabbed the
soap and scrubbed herself roughly, letting the suds cover
her whole body. The dirt drifted away as she eased her
body lower, slowly turning the water brown.

The damselfly buzzed in a shallow circle. The light passed
through its translucent wings, down to the small brook and
back up; on and on into the galaxy. The insect landed
lightly on a leaf a few inches from the water and saw the
world through the thousands of squares of its compound
eyes. A toad leapt straight for the insect, mouth gaping.
The damselfly lights off instantly, and the toad finds only
air. The damselfly flies up in a slow moving arc, tracing
the path of infinity. And straight into a large spider web.
Its panicked struggles only serve to entangle and lock the
insect in. The spider feels the vibrations and climbs out its
burrow. With eight foggy eyes it heads straight for its
prey. But when the spider gets close the damselfly
savagely eats it. The damselfly stops its struggling and
calmly waits on fate. Whether a stronger animal comes
along or it slowly starves to death, the spider in its belly
will give it a few extra hours. The mark of all great
predators is the will to live.

48.   Sit, Little Puppy. Stay. Good Dog.

I lost my way for a bit. Couldn't sit in this chair without going insane. Lost all will for life and understanding when faced with the vast cavern of death. The universe lies in eternal darkness dotted only with brief blocks of light. A false brightness. But now the possibility. Black holes into white and the other side of space. An eternal light universe with only galaxies of beautiful darkness. What an interesting world. Twisted and beautiful. The perfect compliment, a mirror image. A body so small sitting here but with the possible mind large and connected. Sit for six hours. Sit until the moss grows. Sit for six lifetimes. I say as I get up to leave. Break through to the other side. Time travelers awake in the darkness will sleep in light forever.

The bells keep ringing and the world keeps turning. Everything swirls around me. Galaxies, toilets; the design's the same. I sit dead like a stone. The rage has been building itself a monument. I want to dig deep. To find the animal that's alive down there. There seems to be a whole kingdom. Quite the party but no one thought to invite the host. Who do I need to get at? Who can stay? Pulling these fiends out, examining them. They're at once executed or stuffed back in. My insides are lined with blue glass. I shatter the casing and let it rebuild. There was too much space between my skin and robot insides. I press the metal to the edge and there is no more room for fear or hurt or panic. I am ready. Ready to cover the distance, ready to die this moment. Or to live forever, whichever comes first.

49. The Worth

Though the sweet escape flashed again in my mind, I would not desert the corpse. The fight must be stayed, if for nothing else, the summer breeze. The pain, heartbreak, heartache, tears and all. For the warm sun and gentle breeze. It is worth all else. Stay with me, must I scream it again, stay with me.

50. Dollar Tuesdays

Two-dollar well whiskey on Tuesday nights. Whoever
thought this idea up should be congratulated and
strangled. Ah Shiva, the true India Pale, destroyer and
bringer of life. The bar was stuck underground through
the back door of some hipster restaurant. It was as dark as
my brain and the walls were crumbling. There were no
windows and only one way in and out. My companion for
the evening was The Chef. He weighs a solid 225 lbs.
Tattoos cover arms made tough from years of farm labor
before his pursuit of the culinary arts. His wife had left
him about two months prior. We'd been living together
two weeks.

    The night was progressing at a moderate pace. About
seven ladies, all of them ugly, were scattered amongst the
cave. I was wearing my bright prom shoes and decided to
play some songs on the jukebox. It wasn't long before the
music was kicking in and the drinks were kicking in and
the socializing was kicking in. We wrangled two of the
women for a game. Things were going well. I excused
myself from a pool table to take a leak. The bathroom was
all the way back down the entrance corridor. The hallway
stretched into eternity, and I thought about bars in the
50's. Places where you didn't go to meet women. You
met women under sober conditions. Or you were
introduced. None of this jungle shit so prevalent now.
Darwin would piss himself. Twelve guys fighting over a
girl you wouldn't give a first glance to in the light of day. I
entered the bathroom to find three queued up. Nothing
more awkward than rubbing elbows in the john. Then
someone decided to take a leak in the sink. I elected not
to wash my hands on the way out.

I made my way back into the cave. My songs were winding down and there was a commotion at the pool table. The Chef had poured a whole beer onto the green felt. Our opponents weren't too happy. The one with the big ass said something as I walked up but I couldn't quite piece it together. I think I'm falling in love. The four things I require in a woman. Big hips, big chest, big heart, big brains. She at least had three of them. Who cares about breasts when it really comes to it? The Chef was waiting on me like a Jehovah's witness set to testify.

"These guys want to fight. Watch yourself." I looked over at the five guys and shook my head. Firstly because The Chef creates violence where none exists. Secondly, I happened to be holding a pool cue. I've heard it called fighting dirty, but I call it fighting to win. I could take out at least 3 before the other two had time to blink. But these five where lambs. I turned back to our two pool opponents and tried to console them about the water hazard on the pool table.

"It's really a pool table now," I said smiling. They didn't laugh at my joke. The bouncer came over with a towel and began blotting up the beer. The Chef made a comment to him. He can't let another big man be, and the bouncer has him by at least fifty pounds. The game and the evening resumed. There is one point in all serious drinking bouts where the scale is tipped. The fun's peaked, all good decisions have been made, and all that's left runs the gamut from bad to worse. Debauchery reaches its fever pitch, and we were clearly on the downward slope of that point. I was engrossed at the small bar with another young lady with coke bottle glasses. Out of the corner of my eyes I see the chef sneaking up behind the bouncer. He wraps his arm around him and lifts him off the ground. The moment freezes in time as I see the weight of the bouncer is too much. He is lifted high and their center of gravity becomes one. The Chef's ankle snaps sideways and they

79

both fall to the ground. The bouncer scrambles up ready to fight but stops and turns pale. Chef's ankle is dangling at an unnatural angle. It looks like cooked spaghetti hanging limply. We set him down on a chair and I say we should call an ambulance. He declines the ambulance ride and I jet out to get my car. The bouncer and one of the five help to carry him out.

We head to the E.R. at three in the morning. I'm mostly inebriated and driving much too fast for the number of cops in this town. But we make it safely to the hospital. I run in and ask for a wheelchair. They wheel him in and I begin trying to convince them he fell down a flight of stairs. For insurance reasons of course. I hadn't had health insurance for twelve years and wasn't exactly sure how it worked. I was fairly certain they could deny you coverage for wounds sustained in bars. The nurses thought I was responsible for the injury and wouldn't let me in the back room. I looked down at my shiny prom shoes and questioned every decision I'd ever made in my life. When it all goes down you want to be sure you're in the right footwear, and these definitely weren't it. After an hour they finally let me back to talk to him. They had pumped him full of painkillers. The doctor explained the injury to me while pushing his ankle into place. It immediately popped back out and the tip of the bone barely poked through the skin.

"Interesting," I say, "Doctor we may have to amputate."

"What you just say?" The Chef slurs out. His voice so deep he sounds like a demon hunter.

"Nothing," I answer. "I'll be waiting outside for you."

He resumes hitting on one of the nurses. She looks uncomfortable and I bust out laughing. They get ready for the surgery and I return to the waiting room. Staring around the room everything has a bit of the hazy glow. The alcohol gives me the warm hug and I settle in for the rest of the morning. To think of everything and nothing all at once, but mostly to wonder about the girl with coke bottle glasses. She could have been the one, and now she's gone.

51.   The Rich Coast

It was Gideon's fifty-eighth birthday and the prostitute was nineteen at best. One thing with Costa Rica, you can fuck a quarter of your age for what you make working a few hours back in the states. He was already breathing heavy walking up the stairs to the small room above the casino. He noticed she was small and dark, with big eyes and skinny arms.

"I'm a fat old man," he thought to himself but smiled inside. The business got started and he was sweating like he just stepped from the sauna. He pumped harder and harder. Gideon had never felt such glory and then the pain started in his arm. He kept going but the room was spinning and he gasped and clutched his heart.

"Born coming out a vagina and going to die going into one," he shouted out and slumped on her.

"How the fuck am I going to get this guy off me," she thought, but in Spanish.

52. Story time

Psychology class was second period. James nervously walked to the front. He met the eyes of Dema and quickly looked down at his paper. He cleared his throat and began reading.

"My god. You are the ugliest man I've ever seen," Genie said to Phineas.

He bowed his head down as if he was a turtle, trying to hide. "It was my papa's fault. He was ugly too."

"I'm pretty sure it was your whore mother," she sneered.

"Raurrgh," Phineas yelled, splashing her with Jim Jones Kool-Aid, "You know I've got a temper bitch."

James looked up at the class.

"The end," he said quietly. A couple students laughed but most just sat there dazed out of their minds. James walked back to his seat and briefly caught Dema's glance again. The teacher was on his eighth cup of coffee and shifted in his seat, "Who's next?" he barked with a surprisingly penetrating voice for such a small man.

53. The Spaceman Returns

Four billion years had passed. His mind had been silent
for the last two million, a perfection of the godmind. The
shape of the universe, a twisted eight. The scientists had
predicted he would take four times as long to get back but
he had looped over on the crossroads. He had seen things
only angels had. Giants in battle and the eye of Heaven.
The long distant races of man and beast. He must have
had the mark because they all let him pass, briefly pausing
in their eternal war to let him through. At the crossroads
of the universe he sailed by four billion souls in the freezer
of purgatory. And right behind the ice laid the eye of
Hell. The fire cusp between the two universes. To pass
through to Heaven, and back to Earth, flowing amongst
the river of souls on the same course he traveled. He
considered every subject in human existence. Thought
fourteen million years on the comedy inherent in human
tragedy. Came up with a thousand new maths and morals.
And finally he was coming back around. The sun was
huge and had eaten Mercury and Venus. His mind recalled
the faint emotion of desire when he thought of Venus, but
it quickly floated away. Half a breath passed and he was
upon the Earth. Most of the moon was gone but what
little remained showed half a check mark. The Earth itself
was only a small dark nugget. The craft headed straight for
the burnt little crispy ball. He saw the flames but couldn't
remember what fear felt like. The craft sped up as it
headed as it neared the burnt husk. The wings melted off
and his last thought before his craft broke apart was joy
and release. If the machine could smile it would have been
grinning. And his soul drifted back up on the same path
he had entered.

54. Rainbows

Nothing seems important to me much anymore. I play
tennis and dream dumb dreams and think about some
things but since I met her nothing else seems to be the
same color. She has sucked the beauty out of the Earth.
All the things that used to shine brightly and would bring
me such joy don't really register much more than middle
gray. It is a sad state. All the suckers and chumps and
foolish lovers I never had reason to anything but laugh at,
I now see sitting beside me and below me and on top of
me. These states are no good. My job is not fulfilling. I
want to be a writer only. To spend the days sitting and
thinking and occasionally spitting a sentence out. And I
work with this idiot grin because I know it will never
happen.

Why such defeatist thoughts? he said.

The year must be considered successful. I have finished
projects and beaten others and been beaten. I've
improved and gotten worse and fuck it's late and this
makes no sense but I must be nearer to the end and that in
itself must be some sort of accomplishment. I'll write
songs to you and hammer nails and break stones and
pretend that it all matters.

Be calm. he said.

Another chance flies by and I go to retrieve it. A dog in
the cage chasing the stick rattling back and forth. What
next? One more opening, another day. A small rest, some
water. And then what? Your heart explodes and you
never got picked for the contest and fuck it all it's over.

You might have had a laugh or been successful or not. Did you rebel? Did you try your hardest or roll over and die? Did you cry? Did the tears burn your cheeks and still did any of it matter? A rainbow is a perfect circle when viewed from the air. I'm at war with myself and can't figure out whether I'm winning or losing.

55. Blind Date

She ate that sandwich like a shark, eyes rolling back in her head to show the whites, the carnage of lettuce and meat and mayonnaise pushing out and falling onto the plate. And then she daintily picked up her napkin and dabbed the corners of her mouth.

"So what do you do?" she asked.

I shuddered, got up from the table, and walked out of the restaurant.

56. The Book of Revelations

And all will be revealed. Some day, my friend, some day.
Or not, who can really say.

57. Dig it

Cullen digs and digs and digs. Since he was twelve years old. He was mostly normal as a young boy, but puberty hit and all he could think of was how to dig. He really got cranking when he was fourteen. His body started to fill out and he could move that dirt.

"What you doing?" his mother asked one day at lunch.

"Building mountains," he answered in between eating four sandwiches.

They lived on a 4000-acre farm in the flats of Iowa and as long as his house chores were done, she left him pretty much alone. His dig site was forty acres from the house and she would bring him lunch occasionally. He was the youngest of six boys and most everything was taken care of by his brothers. When he dug, he would go into a trance, his eyes glazing over. He worked like a machine, over and over. He dug all day. When he took a rest to look over his progress, he admired the pill bugs most. Their hard shell bodies so strong and just like him they never seemed content. They were always exploring the upturned worlds he created. He liked the way they shapeshifted to the perfect ball when he touched them and wondered if they felt fear.

Down and down he dug. He altered between pick and shovel. His hands became like the rocks he bore thru. His back soon full of iron rods. His older brother who knew carpentry showed him how to shore up tunnels, the side, and build his ladders. By the time he was sixteen he could dig no further down. He had struck large rocks before but this was different. He started back from the beginning. When he had finished he had a massive hole, 30x30, three stories down. He started tunneling out in every direction. A little mouse digging his own maze. Tunneling and shoring up as he went. He built a large room underground, changed the wood to cement and moved himself in. Like the pillbug in the tunnel, Cullen finally felt safe. He spent more and more time in his hole, making the cave into a home. Two of his brothers went off but the others remained, and they still took care of most things.

The end came slowly at first, like the tide inching higher every year, but then soon turned to a rogue wave. He was happy to welcome his family into his bunker. He couldn't have dug deep enough though. The ground was on fire and the wind pulled the earth up, exposing his roof. The fire and rock rained down and tore holes in his burrow. He looked up to see an angry sky the color of a furnace. He tried to tighten up like a pillbug and curl together into a ball. And though his muscles were like iron, he had shed his exo-skeleton 400 million years back. And the last thing he noticed was not even the pill bugs were surviving as his flesh opened like butter being pierced from a knife.

58. My My My

Fleas.
I consider my tie with the greats.
Fleas in my bed.
No escape my fate.
I scratch my polka dot sleeves.
Fleas.

59. The Pilot

The Biology book screamed at Lucas Culder. The final
loomed tomorrow and notebooks were due. The
notebook alone counted as twenty percent of the final
grade. A thick textbook and two spiral loose leafs lay open
on his desk. All around the books tiny plastic pieces lay
strewn about. The model airplane sat half-finished on his
dresser. It would someday be a 1928 Ford Tri Motor. The
plane was the Model-T to commercial airlines in the 30's.
The stout plane was all metal construction. Its fuselage
and wings boasted aluminum alloy corrugated for extra
strength. It featured eleven wicker seats and in-cabin
heaters. An aviation revolution at the time.

Lucas looked at the open model kit, and then back to
his textbook. His notebook for the past six weeks was a
study in stream of consciousness writing; the pieced work
of a first rate daydreamer. He had borrowed Charlotte's to
copy. She never missed a word from their teacher's
mouth. Lucas stood and walked to the model kit. He
fingered the tiny plastic pieces, admiring the little man he
knew would be the captain. The pilot was soft gray plastic,
about the size of a kidney bean. He wore an Eskimo fur
coat and thick trousers. He possessed the calm dead eyes
of a hero. Lucas set him on the edge of his dresser and
went back to his desk. He resumed reading and made
about four sentences before looking over. There sat the
little captain gazing at him.

"I know you need your airplane," Lucas said. "How
else will the people get back to Chicago in this snow?" He
turned and read a few more sentences. "Demit captain,"
he said without looking up. "This is the 21st Century, we
must have a fundamental understanding of our own

human makeup. I know these people have lives; I know the airline has schedules. I'm a pilot myself. But nowadays pilots must know biology." He buried his nose into the book and read two sentences from inches away. He lifted his head and looked again at the small figure. The captain sat patient. Lucas tossed his head back. "Aargh," he growled.

He picked up the biology book and threw it across the room. Its covers spread open and gracefully achieved lift before slamming into the wall and sliding down to a pile on the floor. He began organizing the small gray pieces into tidy rows. He set out his glues and paints, and then arranged his brushes and tweezers in rows like soldiers. He set a jar of water and a few paper towels on top of the notebooks. The little captain watched in silence. He cracked all the lids and the room quickly filled with the smell of paint and glue and purpose as the night crept on.

Biology was first period, and Lucas's eyes burned raw. Someone had parked a train inside his skull. The students who walked by caught the faint hint of model glue. It was nothing unusual for Lucas, and no one looked twice. Charlotte came in. She was sophomore skinny with brown hair and baby blue eyes. She walked over and stood next to his desk.

"Wow you look rough, can I have my notebook back?" Lucas grimaced and pulled the notebook from his bag. It was soaked thru with water, covered in paint and glue.

"What happened," she asked as she touched it lightly. The papers were dissolving under her fingers.

"I accidentally forgot it was on my desk when I was putting my model together. I must have fallen asleep and knocked my water over last night. I'm so sorry, it doesn't make up but I want you to have this."

He pulled the Tri-motor from his bag. It was a thing of beauty. Light and delicate, the glue and paint still tacky to the touch. The aluminum gray sparkled next to the bright black of the airplane's nose. The propellers easily turned with a touch and the landing gear spun as well. The small captain stared out of the cockpit, his gaze solid and ready. Charlotte carefully took the plane and examined it. She looked the aircraft all over with the eye of an engineer and then brought it up to eye level. She peered in the cockpit at the tiny pilot. She broke eye contact and spun one of the propellers. Charlotte made a small banked turn with the plane. Lucas noticed a tear slide down her cheek.

"You're filth, " she said slamming the plane down with fury on the linoleum floor. She stomped it twice with her foot and then rushed to her seat, the notebook coming apart in her hands. Lucas felt a sick emptiness as he stared at the mangled wreckage of the plane. And then he saw the pilot in the middle of the refuse. He picked up the little plastic man. The rest of the class was staring at him but Lucas made no eye contact. He brushed the demolition under his seat and focused his eyes on the nothingness inches from his face.

The teacher entered the room with a stack of crisp white papers. "Notebooks up and pass these back," he said as he handed out the test packets. Lucas took one for himself before passing the stack over his shoulder. He looked at the small man in his hand, then discreetly put the pilot in his mouth and swallowed. The captain felt like a rock sliding into his belly as he penciled his name in the corner of the still warm paper.

60. Appetites

I hunger for something sweet; candy, a woman, a bullet.
This line, already I have said too much.
Every woman from my past, I see, and am filled with
relief; we did not become we. Is every desire simply a lie
wrapped tight? When I die and come to rest on
humanity's road, the thought makes me content. When
my body becomes dust and stuck to the traveler's bare
feet, I am finally at peace. How wonderful this life can be.

What excuse can I make? There is none. I have been this
way since I was a wee one. Always liked to tinker. If there
were a screw I would turn it. Just pulled it apart.
Electronics were my favorite. I would dismantle things
and look inside of the world of the mid 80's electronics.
As I grew older I continued, only the systems were much
bigger and more complex. I don't know why I never
learned to put things back together. Occasionally I would
try but mostly they didn't work. Let others do that work.
Some people are built to dismantle the world. Reverse
engineer possibly? We'll see as the saying goes. Which my
father said more than anything else. And I always
wondered what he did see.

61. Forever Melting

Eat a popsicle, pet the dog, read death poems. Fall in love,
watch a movie; about death. Have another popsicle, pet
the dog, go to work, die; resurrect. Drink a beer, fall
out of love.
Eat the dog, melt a popsicle, make a movie; about life.

And the days just fall away.

62.   The Shade of the Mushroom

"Cigarette?" she asked. Her hair was an unnatural orange color. Almost neon, and her lips were painted to match.

"No I gave it up."

"Pussy?"

"Gave it up." He stared deep back into her eyes. He didn't know why she was messing with him. They were the same people sober, with different lives in the bottle. They'd been walking the earth alone and independent, growing thick and tough and hard. On loners it's always going to be rough. Some things can't be changed. When you step from the tribe, you step from security.

"Money?"

"Nah I gave it all up."

"Life?"

He just shook his head slowly

"Well then what the hell do you want?"

"I want to wake up and it all make sense. I want to have that calmness, that deadness, that rock of a mind that others can crash into and break against. I want that purpose."

"Maybe you should start waking up before two o'clock in the afternoon," she said.

"Why? The darkness is where creation occurs. Seeds sprout in life, babies are born in the dark."

"Yes but to truly grow they must be brought into the light."

"Well what about the deep sea creatures?" he asked, "never seeing light in 70 million years."

She cocked her head, "They'll burn like the rest when the ocean catches fire."

Maybe she had a point. He couldn't stop making grimace faces.

97

"My cheeks are starting to hurt," he thought. "I don't know if it's what you're saying or me thinking about what you're saying. Or the drugs? Well yeah, it could be those. All these new connections in our brains. A new path but the bridge is out for a thousand others. There'd better be some good connections then. Mushroom connections are always the best. Well except for meditating a lifetime away in some cave. Just take the shortcut. When the snow drip hits and your brain is propelled up one level, great truths are revealed which are always forgotten in the morning. " She broke his line of thinking when she laid her body gently down on top. He felt her hips poking into him like two starting points of truth. He wrapped his arms around her neck and squeezed his eyes together like a child trying to hide. His mouth opened and their breath became one. And still none of it made sense but he knew it didn't matter anymore.

63.   The Memories Live Forever

John's skin and eyes reflected the walls of his apartment. Black and white, gray, and a thousand shades of yellow. He was as wrinkled as the neatly clipped and arranged paragraphs. They lined the walls in every room. And the ceilings. And the floors. The apartment became a cheaply wrapped newspaper present from the inside. The stories were with him always, along with the souls of the departed. He kept his favorites front in his thoughts.

Karen Walker, mother of three, lost her fight to ovarian cancer at the age of thirty-seven. She stroked his hair anytime he felt apprehensive. Sergeant Drake, a real man and a friend if he ever had one. Died in his bed at the age of 88. The Sergeant always called him Johnny. They laughed together on most days. He never forgot that first story Drake told him,

He was holding me like a baby, but I'm a full-grown man. I didn't say anything, just watched him as the blood ran out. I could see the light going fuzzy and feel my body convulse. I tried to squirm but he held me tighter. A tear rolled down his dirty face. I looked around at the destruction and bodies and hands and feet and smelled my skin and felt his burnt hands bleeding with mine. I didn't want him to feel alone so I cried a tear too. Two tears from two bodies in the middle of the desert somewhere between Hell and shopping malls and the real American nightmare. And then I closed my eyes and left him alone.

And that's how I should have died, said the Sergeant, but that's how he died. John patted his shoulder as he cried. June Black was one of the smallest. A toddler just taking her first steps who one night stopped breathing in her crib. Johnny loved when she waddled up to him and sat on his lap in the early morning sun. He would read today's stories to her as she made soft happy little noises.

He spent his afternoons quietly padding around the apartment, reading and remembering. Or climbing his ladder to tape a new story to the ceiling. His nights were kept busy getting to know the new residents, another thousand souls kept alive by his remembering.

A small paragraph was written in the newspaper about the accident. All the apartment residents survived but one. The fire consumed his unit quicker than the rest. The obituary a couple pages after only said John Doe passed and a date. A few read but within weeks no one remembered. And his mind grew dark and he was finally alone.

64. God Yawns

These things we may never know as the Earth spins slowly through space. A pin drop lost in the back of a noisy concert hall. But who heard it? Someone must have heard it or felt it or please god somebody tell me it all matters. Tell me it all matters for something through all this noise. Even to meld with the notes being played. This feeling must pass. Somebody tell me it will pass. Somebody tell me anything, God why aren't you talking or am I not listening? Tell me something, give me a smile, a pat. The least I would do for a dog. Give me something. A desert for these tears, a grave for these bones. What do I need to learn? Is it about love or about money or time? Do I need more discipline? Can I promise you something? I look for meaning in my tasks but perhaps that is all distraction and the tasks simply keep me from staring down the eternal gullet of this yawning monster. I remind myself that if matter exists then God can exist. He probably just has a busy week or something.

65.   15-30 second set

I crack the stone, which was really an egg. It breaks and falls away easily. The smell is horrid. Death and tears, fear soured. There are not four elements, or 212, there are two. Space and electrons. And that might be one element too many. All vibrations, create and destroy, there is no difference? One wavelength, Polar frequencies. Only humans can upset the balance, piling the scales one way or the other, but the balance is there. Neither can be eliminated entirely. Value is in having the thing the other person doesn't. The thought, the material, the woman. I speak to amuse, to educate, to build gold/god, and to pass the time. To see my thoughts in the day.   I would create a language just to tell you to listen.

I hear something.

You must feel the vibration. All the electrons bombard your body at once. Guide them around like an ancient aikido master. Don't fight them. Sift the ones' that mesh, mold the two's you think you need, send the rest away. Someone else can use them. There are only two, the high and low and trillions in between are all just suits for the two. It's raining gifts, purple eggs, like thoughts. I don't even have to crack them open.

Mars Wilder felt many eyes on him and looked around. The line judge was staring at him and behind the judge a child was staring at his ice cream cone. His head shuddered like he was cold and then he remembered where he was. The big man across the net was serving. Drifted from the Cincinnati quarterfinals to infinity. The ball comes up and the big man loads his body and unleashes the ball. It comes over the net at 132 miles per hour and slow like a planet. Back to no thoughts he drifts into eternity's river.

Eggs falling down, the man keeps sweeping up the shells without a thought. So brutish, even if he wears a tie, a monster with a half noose still hanging. Who cut him down? I decide to string him back up, so I may collect some eggs. And with fluid motion Mars connects with the serve and sends it flying back over the net as the crowd holds their collective breaths.

66.   Three Seconds in the Third World

The brush of a breast along my back, when the young lady had plenty of space to walk around. I turn and glance at her gypsy ass. I look up to see her eyes and she flashes me a smile. A thing more beautiful than the Earth and all art I've ever seen. Dark eyed vagabond. Her legs like sycamores from a life of wandering. These are the glimpses of joy, the tastes of life. Brown bananas, unimagined views, trash piling up every day, old stooped men eating watermelons, throwing toothless grins at old stooped ladies displaying legs much too wrinkled for anyone but the watermelon eaters. This energy courses through my body and my slight smile hides my strength to destroy the whole world and build a new one.

67. Strays of Hope

Caul slowly climbed down the ladder and onto the stairs. His breath gathered before him and then crept back, disappearing into his face. He eyed the tile in the foyer and took the first step south.

"Sweet Jesus, give me some warmth," a shout bounded through the house.

"Little early for preaching," he thought to himself, shaking his head and examining the staircase. Rushing down, his bare feet cleared the last step and landed solidly on the white tile. The ice grabbed straight for his groin and his breath came in ragged drags. He stood like a statue until his teeth began knocking and then promptly toppled over into the carpeted living room. Clawing his way to the one square of sunlight coming through the window, he curled into a ball and lay with eyes alive listening to the rest of Joshua's sermon.

A gray and white ball of fur padded in from the kitchen. It sat down softly and stared at Caul on the living room carpet. Duke had been pulled from a box on the side of the road. He was small but wide, sloe-eyed and hungry. Thomas O'Really was the other cat residing in the old house on Ruby Avenue. Thomas came from a lineage of misfortune as dark as her fur. She'd been walking in the graveyard since birth, and having a male name would be the least of her future calamities. Completing the animal kingdom was Joshua's dog Bailey, a purebred retriever. The dog was bought at a very cheap price for being somewhat stunted at birth. She was good-natured though, runt or not.

Joshua walked into the room with a small dishtowel draped around his midsection. He was six foot with muscles cut.

"We've got to get that water heater fixed. I could handle it if there was a little water pressure but you're under there for eternity trying to get the soap off." Caul stared, turning over the fact he hadn't had a shower in four days. Duke rubbed against Joshua's leg, leaving a sparse gray sock of cat hair around the wet ankle. He swore and kicked the animal a few feet into the room.

"Did I tell you what that little junkie did to me last night? I grill a nice tuna fish sandwich, set it on my plate, and go to get a drink out of the refrigerator. I swear not more than ten seconds. Turn back around and he's up on the table, towering over the sandwich and staring at me. The little dirt bag never takes his eyes off me, calmly lifts up a paw and places it directly in the middle of my sandwich. I threw him clean across the kitchen into the wall." Josh took a breath, "What's your problem?" Caul continued staring, thinking about the chocolate bar incident.

"My problem?" he answered. "Is I'm listening to a half naked lunatic jabbering about throwing small animals into walls at seven thirty in the morning. I can watch my breath in here even though it's sixty degrees outside, and this whole place stinks of cat piss. The sofa that's been on the front porch for two months smells better than the one in here. Christ-o-matic, we really need to examine what choices led to this?" Caul pulled himself up, grabbed his cigarettes off the coffee table and walked out the battered front door. "The sweater of my civilization has gone to the moths," he thought to himself as a match sparked to life. His brown hair stuck out in all directions and his flannel pajama bottoms had cigarette burns from smoking in bed. Pulling his toes underneath him, the little chief sat on the plaid green couch and realized with certain determination it was a beautiful morning.

Josh walked out a few minutes later, trailed by his life partner. Caul looked up, "So what're you into today?"

"Eh, figured I'd go to the park with Bailey, maybe swing by the music store, I don't know, go on a jog."

"A jog might be a good idea, flesh vault," he said, "Even Bailey's looking a bit thick."

"You going to work?"

"I figured I'd show up for a couple hours," Caul answered.

"Alright, lates homie," he said as they hopped in his truck.

Caul pulled himself off the couch and threw some clothes on. The drive to Asheville lasted about twenty minutes. He was helping remodel a house a friend had bought some months ago. And even though he hadn't the slightest idea what he was doing, he still enjoyed the work. He wasn't at work long before his phone rang. It was Dabney; the untouchable, the queen. "Hey, just thought I'd tell you, my sister found a dog, it's pretty nice, all white, blue eyes, thought you might want it." "

"Boy or girl?"

"Girl," she answered.

"Where'd she find it?"

"The road near exit fifty five."

"She have to cage it?"

"No, been running around the yard with her dogs, she already went and got its shots too."

"Alright, I'll have a look, you busy today?" he asked.

"No, you want to meet at your house?" she said.

"Yeah, give me half an hour."

Caul quickly cleaned up at the house and locked up. This was something. Something indeed. Dog to warm the bed. Dog to eat cats. Dog Almighty, this could be the turnaround. He sped back home, flew off exit sixty-five and the last mile to the house. He sat on the couch outside chain smoking till the white Honda pulled in the drive. Dabney hopped out.

"Hey what's going on," her voice had a soft country twang. She waved as she pulled the back door open. She was wearing jeans that looked designed for her figure, and he wondered how a plain white t-shirt could look so good. He was on to admiring her kink blonde hair and then all his attention turned. Like a wild stallion the great beast hopped out the car, blue eyes burning. Caul's breath caught in his stomach. He got up and slowly walked to the dog. He extended his hand and let it sniff. Running his hand down the animal, he could feel the spine pressing into his hand, and the bones of its haunches.

"Yeah Dabney, I think this will work out," he said. They stood around talking for a few minutes, but Caul's mind was wandering. Normally Dabney would be the only thing on his. She must have sensed this and took her leave.

The two stood in the yard staring at each other with the sun coming down as the gnats circled like planets. "Guess you'll be wanting something to eat," Caul said to the dog. The dog stared back. He put the dog in the passenger side of his truck and drove to town. Food, bowls, flea medicine, collar, leashes, and a doggie brush. The animal was left inside to guard the truck. Caul smiled to himself, pride full, as walking across the pet store parking lot they locked eyes. When the two got back to the house Joshua was out in the yard with Bailey.

He climbed out of the truck and then opened the door for the dog. The white beast immediately gave Joshua the once over and Bailey the twice. The dogs began chasing each other around. A warm-up, Caul would later reflect.

"So that's that, huh," Joshua asked.

"Yeah, I thought I'd call her Claude. Or maybe Zebulon," Caul answered.

"Thomas O'Ralley's going to lose it with two dogs in the house," said Josh. "I just hope your dog eats that little bag." Caul fetched the dog food and accessories out of the truck. He walked inside the house and filled up the food and water. Walking back out, he grabbed his dog and led it towards the door. At the threshold the animal started pulling back. Caul swore as he pulled on the leash, but the dog wouldn't budge.

"I know the things hungry, I'm going to get the food and lure it in," he said walking in the door. Grabbing the bowl, he came back through the living room.

"Zebulon just ran down the street," Joshua said as Caul stepped out. The dog was three houses down, sniffing around. He broke into a brisk jog, straight for the animal. When he was within five feet, the dog broke and ran around the house. Caul bolted after the beast. He came near and dove but the dog sidestepped and he landed facedown on the ground. The chase became a well-timed game. Caul slowed down, the dog agreed and took a breather, he sprinted, and Zebulon sprinted. Around houses, over hedges, trees, parked cars. The dog made one error and Caul grasped his tail with a lunge. But the animal was strong and jerked herself free. Eventually they came to the end of the street. The dog crossed the pavement and disappeared down a dirt road. Caul was about 40 feet behind and at the dirt road in seconds. He skidded to a stop at the start of the road and eyed an over-weight lady and her little dog standing in the corner yard staring through him.

"Excuse me ma'am," he asked, "you see a white dog run by here?"

" 'at's Sheila's dog," she bawled back.

"Um, that's Claus," he answered.

"No, 'at's Sheila's dog alright, she run off about a week ago. 'at girls been crying her little eyes out ever since."

Caul shifted from one foot to the other, as the plump lady and her small sidekick continued boring holes into him. "Well hell," he muttered. "Tell her I'm glad she got her dog back." He slowly turned and started walking back down the road to the little green house on Ruby Avenue, head hanging. Caul saw Joshua's Chevy coming down the road. The truck slowed to a stop and he climbed in.

"Lose your dog?" Josh asked.

" 'At's Sheila's dog," he disgustingly spit out. They drove down the road and Caul relayed the events. As they neared the end of the street, the trucks headlights fell upon what must be Sheila and the great white beast. She had a stranglehold on the animal and was fastening some kind of chain to his collar. Caul rolled the window down and poked his head out. The woman was hysterical.

"Hey, that your dog? My friend found it down in Swannanoa."

"Robby said either I go or the dog does, and I was going leave him, but then I had to go to work, and when I got back, Snowflake was gone and he said she must of broke her chain and got loose. I've been tore up all week, not knowing what happened to her. This ain't her collar, and she looks skinny but-"

Caul cut her off "glad you got your dog back." As the three were pulling away they could still hear her rambling about how things would be different and dog miracles. For a second the animal and Caul's eyes met and they flashed defiant, and then the dog threw his head up like a horse. The car was silent as they drove slowly down the road.

Finally he looked over to Joshua, "Damn, I still say that's the best dog I ever had." They both busted out laughing and were soon on to other matters as they drove the last few miles into town. A rusty Ford Taurus passed them and shortly turned down the gravel driveway. Robby heavily pulled himself out of the car. He stumbled to the trailer and through the front door. "My God," he swore and took a step straight for Snowflake as Sheila got up screaming.

68. On Your Marks

He was seven years old and pedaling furiously. Riding that rusty one speed with the racing banana seat. He rounded the corner, wind whipping through his Mohawk. He saw his mom and raced right for her. He mashed his left foot down hard and whipped the back tire around into a perfect power slide. He was smiling ear-to-ear as the gravel parted ways and sprayed out before him. He slid for what seemed like days and knew she would be proud. And then that smile turned to angst when he saw his mother's face. Pure hatred and violence distorted the shape as she began yelling at the top of her lungs. He pulled his shoulders up to his ears as she clamped around his skinny wrist, yanked him off the bike, and pulled him into the house.

69. Mishmash

I should be writing but decide to shine every shoe in my
closet. Then string a few tennis rackets. Then read a
book, then watch some television, clean my room, take a
nap, overthrow the government. My whole life, lost within
the should. These decisions I've made. At best idiotic, at
worst, insane. I go for the most complicated way about
things. The simplest answer was always to make the
money first and then go for the adventures. But I could
never manage the simple. And this is how I found myself
looking through a peephole waiting for that big Neo-Nazi
to come pounding through the door.

I was working in Raleigh as a stonemason.
Something about the work almost calmed my restless
insides. The rows and rows of neatly ordered bricks or the
wild jigsaw of rough cut stone. My forearms had always
been big but after working for a year lifting block and
hauling mortar they were massive. The company boss was
a golf fanatic. He would regularly cut out to play eighteen.
It was a small company and we soon ran out of work.
After a couple weeks my money was drying up. I could
have gotten another job but I was never real keen on the
idea in the first place. I'm a writer. If I were prone to
working I'd be in another line of work. Plus those
forearms made me think I could do anything. So with rent
coming and credit cards five months due the obvious
solution was to sell my nice truck, vacate the apartment,
and move into a van. A romantic notion for a stationary
and trapped wanderer.

Once I started looking it was soon apparent a station
wagon would be a more hip option. I found one close. It
was a beauty, old and immaculate. But on the test-drive
the owner started fish tailing around corners in his long

dirt driveway and the transmission slipped. He promised it was nothing and he would fix the car. So I kept looking. Soon I was searching far across the country. Colorado seemed to have the 70's station wagon market cornered. I found a couple I liked and got set on one. It was a 68 Impala. White with red wheels. We started emailing and the owner promised there was nothing wrong with the car, ready to drive and solid enough to make it back the 1700 miles. I tried reaching the Raleigh guy again but no answer. Three days and he didn't call me back. So I sold the truck to my dad. The fact I had borrowed money from him to buy in the first place did not escape my mind. Don't think I had ever paid it back either. Prodigal son in the new millennium, the scumbag runs deep in me.

I bought the plane ticket to Denver. The first snowstorm of the season beat me there by a few hours. I had no jacket and stepped off the plane wearing a t-shirt. The owner picked me up in a little Honda Civic and we drove into downtown. His name was Wayne. He was a pale six foot, at least 220, and bald as a cue ball. He gave me a long sleeve shirt to wear and we drove straight to the car. The outside looked good but the interior was rough. Went to turn the key and it wouldn't start. We tried jumping it off but with no luck.

"It must need a new ignition coil," Wayne said, "I know a mechanic." We pushed it a half mile through the snow. The mechanic was an old black guy. He looked hesitant about fixing it. "I don't know about working on a snow day." I had to beg him but he ended up agreeing to the work.

Wayne suggested we go to the bar while we waited for the repairs. We walked there. He pointed out to me his boots left little swastika's imprinted in the snow. The bar was a little local's only shithole. I ordered a boilermaker to try and warm up. Wayne pulled a large hunting knife out to pop the top of his beer bottle. He said he was from a small town about thirty minutes outside where I'm from. He slowly revealed to me he was a reformed Neo-Nazi, still believed but didn't associate with the guys anymore. Said they were getting too crazy. He showed me his large 'SS' and personal gang tattoos. Don't know if he knew Caleb was a Jewish name or not. It means 'dog' roughly translated. Supposed to represent loyalty I think. I was starting to wonder if the station wagon held some hidden things from white power. We finished up and headed back to the mechanic. I paid the bill in cash, about two hundred dollars. Wayne said we needed to go pick up the title. We drove about thirty minutes outside the city to retrieve the document. We finally made it back to the car. I got to drive it as darkness was falling. The brakes were going to the floor. It needed a new master cylinder. We drove to a hotel and I went to get a room.

"I need a minute to think about it," I said.

I put my stuff in the hotel room and sat for two minutes. I wanted the wagon but the lies about its condition bugged me. And I knew buying from a Nazi, new or old, would haunt me. I walked back outside and told him no. I said don't worry about the repair bill. I noticed his face turning a bright red and his forehead tightening up in anger. I turned and walked back into the room. My heart was pounding. I pressed my body up against the hotel door and looked out the peephole. He was sitting in his car fuming. I was worried I would have to fight him. He was big and I'd be in the hospital or dead. The seconds felt like hours. I couldn't feel the hand of God and my feet were freezing. I didn't know anyone in this town and my thoughts kept flashing up the hunting knife buried deep in my breast. I pulled away from the door and plotted my best defense. When I carefully checked the peephole again he had driven off. I can only imagine it was my forearms. I let out a sigh that lasted hours and sat back on the bed still shaking. I sat in the room feeling more alone than I ever had. I lost all hope for the first time in my life in that La Quinta Inn in Denver. I submitted an old piece to a short story contest that night. Of course it didn't win but I still set myself to write the next one.

In the morning I took a cab to the bus station. I purchased a ticket to Colorado Springs. There was another wagon for sale there. I sat waiting in the station and missed the Greyhound. I thought they would announce departure and it pulled up ten minutes early. I wouldn't have thought buses left here without passengers, being as how I've never rode a bus in America. The ticket agent didn't say a word. Just watched the whole thing. I took a cab to Colorado Springs. The cabbie cut me a deal and talked more than anyone I'd ever met. His biggest fare he'd ever had was three illegals going to Cleveland. Almost three thousand dollars. He told me a story about two Australian bank robbers who left 136,000 dollars in a bag in a trashcan in the airport. He had a four-year degree in criminal studies, and a minor in chinchinta something or another. In the news yesterday a van flipped carrying sixteen people. Four died. At least we haven't wrecked in the snow yet. I checked into a motel and tried contacting the local owners. The guy in Colorado Springs wouldn't call me back. But I did finally receive a message from Raleigh, "The wagon is good to go, just a hose came loose. Running like a dream." I groaned. The die was cast. Life is tough when you have no patience. So I went to the bar in Colorado Springs. I had a few beers and a woman took me back to the hotel but nothing happened.

I tried calling Cleveland the next morning about a green Ford wagon and hitching a ride there. I must have been giving off the desperation scent though because I wasn't getting calls back. I was on the edge by that point anyways. Hotels, food, and cabs quickly add up; and my money stack was shrinking. I rented a car and went back to Denver and bought a rusted out piece of shit wagon for 1200 dollars. A 1977 Chevy, ugly gold, with interior in bad shape. But it made it back no problem. And it would have been a sweet ride remodeled. I attempted, but that's a separate disaster for another time. I have a knack for underestimating things. I drove back in two straight days, through snow and storm. Hallucinates came on as I drove down a mountain in West Virginia. Started seeing figures both in the road and alongside as I argued with God. I knew the trip was a disaster. He spoke to me and told me to pull over and tell him face to face. I turned around and took a little side road. I can't remember if I was arguing, accusing, or just talking. The recall is hazy. I sat waiting for God on the lonely road. Suddenly a car turned appeared over the hill. I got spooked. I wasn't ready to be smited. I jumped in and drove back to the highway, apologizing to God for the next three hours. I was soon back in Raleigh and my life there. But now with more proof of my foolish choices. I always wondered if God was really in that car. We started working construction again the next week, like the past had never happened. I look in the mirror and see a man-child with no ability to see the probabilities that lie within the possibilities.

70. Royalty

Once there lived a young girl, who knew she would grow to be queen. So she spent her days doing royal things. And when she was grown, she was indeed the queen. But no young boys had felt the same dream. And after all that, she was the saddest queen to have ever lived.

71.   The Worker

I licked my callous.
Felt strange on my tongue.
I could taste my life,
and everyone's.

72. Galaxy 19

Colony logbook 42: Chapter 7463. Day 38.

We were the last of the human survivors. Galaxy 19 in the
Seventh-Wave colonizing mission. All the rest had met
with misfortune. Space travel is dangerous. Like walking
through a stranger's house in the dark. If that stranger
owned a pack of heavily armed giant tigers. There are just
too many things that go bump. Asteroids, brutal life
forms, and time collapses were some of the things that had
met the early expeditions. And then the birth even
slammed through the universe. The folding and unfolding
of creation and destruction together took out most of the
remaining humans. The Earth must be long gone by this
point. We were lucky to be exploring one small corner of
the universe. It was on the edges of the unfolding and
didn't receive the full force.

437 generations in space and we looked like the space
aliens of old. Our skin had become translucent. Life in
the dark had made our eyes grow huge and our bodies
wither away. Cranial widening procedures have allowed us
to grow bigger brains. Downloading content straight into
the brain makes every generation smarter than the last.
We only have to foster creativity. We are self sufficient to
a point but still bound by the laws of nature. And now on
one of the last habitable planets, perhaps there will be
another few thousand years for the human race. Life
always remains in the galaxy, but we humans are unique.
Who knows what will come after? There is nothing so
patient as the universe. A sense of hope and excitement is
still within us as we explore our new planet. It is harsh but
will have to do. It will take our bodies generations to feel

any sort of comfort. Our ship fleet is stationed on the perimeter but running out of energy. The unfolding destroyed too much. The sun here is weak but should sustain our early efforts at life. We set the magnets in place and use the last of our energy to kick-start the atmosphere. The most interesting thing, our trackers picked up an unmanned probe on a set course hurtling past us. We tried contact but received no message in return, only computer code for 800,000 years of unbroken laughter. We don't have the energy to chase the probe anyways. So we do what humans have always done through existence. We begin anew.

73. Phone Call

"So what did he say?"

"He didn't really say nothing."

"What do you mean he didn't say nothing? Everybody says something."

"I mean he just sat there looking hurt. His eyes were watering."

"So he didn't say nothing?"

"He said one thing."

"What was that, I knew he said something. Everybody says something."

"Said people with money like you shouldn't buy people presents like that."

"Money like me? I've got half the money he does. I thought he liked them rough, it was his birthday."

"He was covered with red marks. She must have been hungry. Some sort of vampire. Three days later and he's still complaining his nose hurts. I guess she came in the room, got him all worked up, and then straightaway bit him on the knob. He screams out but that was just the beginning. Proceeded to gnaw on him for half an hour while fucking his brains out."

"Oh Jesus, I'd never do that on purpose. He's got to know that."

"I'd just watch your back for a bit, I think the deal is still good but you never know what he might do."

I hung up the phone and walked back into the cabaret. I sat down and sipped my whiskey. I slicked my hair back and stretched my neck forcibly. And then the little dancer locked eyes on me. She jumped off stage and came to my table.

"Vincent?"

"Yeah what about it?" I said.

She laid into my leg with all her might.

"What the fuck was that for?" I said grabbing my thigh.

And she kept on. Those little fists over and over. "Gio said you never do that to someone. Gio said business is business but now you put in a personal level? Said he's going to send someone over to have lunch on your dick."

I was dressed too nicely to have this dwarf yelling at me. And then she was on top, unleashing a flurry of punches. She was really making a scene, and those little hits started to hurt.

"Hey, hey, you guys," I looked to my big men but they just turned their backs. I was going to kill those sons of bitches when I got her off me.

74.   We Both Have Eyes but I See More

This is what redemption looks like. A 30-year-old pickup truck. The rust is rusting, the whole mass slowly returning to the earth. The bed is showing through to the road, it rains in the cab when the water comes down outside. God splashing you with the holy water. This is redemption. This is what it looks like when you slam rock bottom, get up and keep digging deeper. Grab the pick ax and start chipping away. Chip, chip, chip, maybe you find some jewels. Maybe you sit back down and turn to dust. Finally you pull yourself up hand by hand, always towards the light, the blue sky and clouds. Your shoulders scream, your muscles burn acid, fingernails popping off, blood and dirt all mixed together. And everything washed by the salty sweat and tears. When you are climbing up, many things can help you a step, and many can knock you back down. And wrapped up in both sits a woman. Salvation and doom, like right and left hands, two eyes in the same head. Either way, life and death are sweet when they come from her. And you pop your head through the clouds for one brief minute, take a large inhale of breath and look around. And then some crab is dragging you back in.

75.   The Dark Angel

The sun beat down on the dusty road. It washed the color
out of life and replaced it with a harsh and unforgiving
pale. The man walking was six feet tall. He wore black
pinstripes that seemed to add another two inches to his
appearance. His shoes once polished were now scuffed
and caked with the brown mud. Sweat dripped thru his
black socks and made his shoes squeak with every step.
His gray shirt was soaked like he'd been swimming. It
clung to his thin frame. He had no hat and his skin baked
and his baldhead peeled under the noon Georgia sun. He
carried a small suitcase in his left hand. He wiped his head
with the crook of his soaked shirt and cursed the heat and
the sky and the dirt. If the sun heard his curse it offered
no remorse. It sat quietly baking, putting the earth to rest.
The man was dressed like Sunday. His name was Aaron,
and he walked without a clear destination, only down the
road. Always down the road. He decided to get off the
road and find the shelter of a tree but nothing except vast,
empty fields greeted his eyes in all directions. He stopped
and wiped his brow and looked at his watch. It was a
weathered timepiece. Silver and gold. Something from
another era, something like himself. He put his arm back
down and continued, one more foot in front of the other.
        He heard the crunch of gravel under tires and turned
to see the wide black car approaching. It drove slowly, as
if the heat held it back also. He stepped to the side of the
road as the car pulled up to him. The sun blinded off the
chrome and he put his hand up to shield his eyes. The
blacked out window lazily rolled down and he was greeted
with the face of a woman in her thirties. Her skin was free

of sweat. The cool air blasted him in the face. She smiled at him but Aaron felt a forced strain hidden inside. Her teeth bright white and perfectly aligned. She had a pale complexion and a small dip in her dress revealed just a hint of cleavage. Like any good man he pretended not to notice.

"Not good for a man to be in the heat like this," the driver said leaning over. He was pushing 300 pounds with a few days stubble. "Where you headed?"

Aaron bent over and regarded the man with no judgments. "Down the road I guess. No where in particular."

"You want to ride a ways? There's nothing out here for the next twenty miles. You have any water? You're as like to die as find some shade."

"I usually do alright, but yeah, thanks for the offer." The woman stepped out. She made eye contact with Aaron and he noticed her face looked more worn in the bright sun. He climbed in the back seat. He set his suitcase in the floorboard. The air hit him and stung his skin. The car was like an iceberg and he shivered violently a few times. They began moving slowly down the road. The interior was dark burgundy leather. Everything wood and chrome and polish. He admired the things man had built and then glanced at the small neck of the lady in the passenger seat. It was thin with the muscles defining and holding the head proud. He thought about this creation man could never build. A building from the blueprints. Life. A creation laid down that self creates. Pretty marvelous in both its complexity and simplicity. And then something called him back. The man's voice it was.

"Where you from my man?" the man asked.

"Everywhere and nowhere," Aaron said with a slight smile.

"You been to Iron City?"

"Can't say that I have."

"So you don't know a soul in this town?" the man asked, his eyes filled the rear view mirror. "What you coming through here for."

"Well that's how you get to know souls," Aaron said.

"What are you looking for?" the man said.

"Something cosmic," Aaron said. "Have to get out the city to see the stars." He grinned big and his teeth looked like large white cubes of sugar.

"Cosmic huh?" The man paused for a moment. "I'll tell you one. The sun is white, you know," he said. "Everybody thinks it's yellow. Nope pure white, it only looks that way from our atmosphere." Aaron looked at the rear view mirror to see the driver's eyes staring again.

"Is that a fact," Aaron said. "I'd have never known."

"That's a fact, all right." They sat in silence for a minute bouncing on the road. Aaron noticed the lady in front shift a few inches. "All of space black as night. Only the pure white light of a sun is worth anything."

"I thought dwarf stars were red," Aaron said. The man's eyes filled the rear view mirror again. His face darkened a shade.

"Some kind of astronomer huh?" he scoffed. "Don't believe all the lies my friend. That was your car broke down back there?"

"Yeah that's mine," Aaron answered.

"It looked like a piece of shit, only a matter of time," the big man said.

"John please," the woman interrupted, placing her hand on the man's arm. The big man looked at her and shook her hand off. Aaron noticed the unmistakable marks on her upper arm. Some looked fresh.

"Well it got me here," Aaron said, "but yeah I think only Jehovah could fix that car."

"I can witness to that," John said and laughed hoarsely. "Afraid that might not be a good thing for you in the long run."

"I've found the long run to be shorter than any of us can imagine my friend." Their eyes met again in the rear view mirror. "You can go ahead and let me out. I appreciate the ride, but I'll probably be better off walking from here."

"Damned if the astronomer don't have a smart mouth."

"Or if the driver don't have dumb ears."

John slammed on the brakes and the car slid to a stop. "You ungrateful son of a bitch. I go out of my way to help you and I hear nothing but insults. You gonna say thank you or should I teach you how?"

"I don't think that would be a good idea for you," Aaron said, his eyes stone cold.

John cut the engine. "One last chance."

"For you or me," Aaron answered.

John jumped out of the car and slammed the door closed. He moved quickly to the trunk. The woman locked the door and turned to him. "He's going to kill you. You can outrun him though, I'm sure of it."

"No one can outrun time," he answered back. The shadow of the big man fell along the outside of the car. He tried to open the door. He roared and slammed his fist into the window.

"Goddam open this door Melissa."

"Open the door," Aaron said.

"I won't do it, he'll kill you." He slammed his fist hard on the window.

"You've got three seconds bitch before I break this window."

"Open the door," Aaron said again.

"I'll drive us out of here," Melissa said. She slid over as the window exploded into a thousand tiny pieces. It cut her face and neck even as she turned away. John reached in and unlocked the door. He drug Melissa out of the car by her hair and tossed her down on the gravel.

"You fucking bitch," he roared. "Out of the car nigger. This ain't my first time cleaning house."

Aaron pushed the seat forward and slowly stepped out. John had a small aluminum bat. Aaron stood to his full height as John reared back and unleashed a swing at his temple. In a flash Aaron swayed back. The bat missed by a fingers width. The swing put John slightly off balance. Aaron stepped towards him. He planted his open hand squarely on his face and it melted around the whole of John's head.

"What you know of the universe is a drop. You humans have grown so smart, yet your compassion is still half dead." Aaron pulled his hand away from John's face. John's mind opened and all his actions lay out in scale. His eyes rolled back in his head and his mouth fell open. He collapsed to the gravel road in a heap. His mouth began opening and closing rhythmically, like a fish out of water, a strange wheeze emitting with each exhale of air. Aaron bent over and looked deep in his eyes. He slowly reached out with his index and lightly touched him again on the forehead. John's massive frame shuddered and slowly began melting into the gravel. He slowly began transferring into a small box turtle. The turtle's mouth continued opening and closing, but with now only a small squeak emitting from its vocal box.

"Who do you think has been protecting me this whole time? I'm on this Earth to learn my lessons too." At this moment an old rusted piece of shit car pulled up alongside and stopped, its motor running like a sewing machine. The driver was darker than Aaron and smiling ear to ear. "Fixed your car. Why the Hell you driving this jalopy?"

"Ran into a string of bad luck," he said grinning and hopped in the car.

"So tell me what bad luck could befall a being like you," the driver said and punched the accelerator. The car pulled off with tires digging. Clouds of dust followed them down the road. Melissa picked herself off the ground and wiped the dust and dirt off. She gingerly touched the glass embedded in her face and blood running down her elbows. She watched the car drive away and then looked down at the turtle. It was staring back at her. She stepped over it and climbed in the driver's seat of the big car. The engine roared to life. She reversed back a few feet until she heard the crunch of the shell under the tire. She rolled down the driver side window and cut the AC off. She let out a big sigh. The car slowly crept down the road while the southern heat baked everything clean like an autoclave.

76.   Ax to the Back, Dream Within a Dream

I awoke from my dreams into a world of zombies. I hid
back in a room and watched a loving couple dismember
each other. My woman came in and I put her to sleep on
the top of the woodpile. I went to go fetch some aspirin
for her headache. I ran down the boardwalk and to a little
store along the way. I found two cops amongst the
grocery aisles. I told them about the zombies. They
looked at me like an idiot speaking Latin and kept on
shopping. A zombie family came in. I snuck up behind
the mother and hit her square in the back with my ax. It
stuck in with a thud. She turned around and gave me a
long hug and didn't seem the least upset about the ax
sticking in her spine. It soon became obvious that people
who are dicks when they're human are still dicks when
they're zombies and kindness remains as well.

77. All the Pieces Fit

It's raining at the U.S. Open. All matches have been
halted and I'm coloring an anatomy book. What's left?
I've been working with the gays. They've been trying to
convince me I'm gay. I went to Tia's house two nights
ago. She was small and soft. Her pelvis kept crushing my
fingers and my hand was cramping up. Her clitoris stayed
covered and wouldn't seem to come out. I had to damn
near pound on it to get her off. Tennis we played the
week before. She wasn't very good at the game, and a
strange one to talk to. Her underwear matched, which I
always appreciate. I got home in the middle of the night,
feeling uneasy in my gut. My roommate's dog was softly
snoring. A lab-pit mix. Friendly as can be, black as night.
I sit now and think is anything worth it. It's a doubt I
can't seem to shake. The jaws are too strong, like an
Alabama tick it's buried deep. An animal that doesn't fit
but isn't smart enough to think its way out. The curse. I
pet the dog and sigh and sleep.

78.   A Proper Lady

"You never loved me," he screamed through mangled lips. Blood and spit dribbled down his chin and he smeared it off and down the front of his dirty t-shirt. The dog lay almost dead in a puddle on the light blue tile. She stared at him but didn't say a word. The blood soaked into her 600 dollar pumps. They were light red and Italian designed. The shoes had been hand stitched in Milan. But her thoughts were not on the shoes as she bent over and picked up the dog. She let out a small grunt as she rose. She could feel the dog's warm blood soaking through her shirt. Plink, plink, a few drops fell onto those perfect little shoes. Tiny drops of rain on the left foot. She squeezed the dog tight to her chest. They'd been together six years. She looked over to him.

"Your heart is empty, nothing but a black hole," she said calmly. Her eyes betrayed no emotion.

She turned and walked down the hall. The plates and glass crunched under her feet. She gently laid the dog in the backseat. She fetched a small shovel from the shed and noticed him staring through the window as she pulled the BMW out of the driveway. She slammed the shifter into drive and peeled off. She sped down the country roads and out into the open. She drove for three hours with jagged edges of thoughts cutting through her brain. She screamed with all her might and her neck stretched up so tight it looked like her trachea would burst.

Finally she pulled off the road. She pulled the dog out of the back seat and drug it away from the road. She laid it gently down. She pulled the shovel off and started digging a hole. The Milan shoes were soon covered in the soft brown Georgia clay. She was sweating heavily and continuously spat in the grave. Finally it was deep enough.

She turned to the dog and pulled her snub nose .38 out. She bent down to pet the dog once more. His chest lightly rose. She aimed at the back of his skull and squeezed the trigger. A hole instantly opened and a spurt of blood jumped out. Never a more succinct picture of cause and effect. She shot the animal four more times in the head and screamed in anguish.

She rolled the dog gently in. She pulled her bracelet and necklace and hairpiece off and threw them in the shallow grave. She spat once more in the grave and started filling it in. When she got back into the car a warm four o'clock afternoon sun fell soft on the earth. She checked the pistol. One bullet in the cylinder and three others in the glove box. That would be more than enough.

79. The Hospital Always Calls. It's Your Birthplace, Please Come Visit.

Another trial passed, but not with flying colors. First Emily, then Charlotte. I connected with both, and have been trying to be a gentleman to both also. How many more will I meet and have to let go? Olivia is in the hospital with a kidney infection. I don't know what to do to make myself better. My hair is falling off my face in patches and thinning on the top of my head. What is it about hospitals that make you feel so powerless? Or is it the illness. Guess I need to give up some things and stop trying so hard in my mind. Try harder in my heart and body. Patience, young one, time is but an illusion. There is only energy, and slowed energy. Olivia has the shakes, nausea, and dry heaves. I have only one lonely soul to give.

80. Just Do It

"They're building it in your day's time," Ehud said to the group of over four thousand Black Hoods. Their proper name was The Nine Black Hoods, but they usually went by the Nine. Wearing masks had been declared illegal but most faces in the crowd were covered. "There was a time when certain things were wrong. They will tell you there is no such thing, that business is you, and business is state. But you are human, and this is the time to realize it. If we don't stop this now all humanity is lost." The crowd parted as he walked off the stage.

He wasn't like the rest. He was the first to break the mind-melds and reverse the programming codes. He had been underground since then. Ehud hadn't received the standard cell transplants in sixty years. The younger ones always asked to touch his face. It was wrinkled and covered in pockmarks. They had never seen such a thing. And he let them. Even though some of them were two hundred years old, they still seemed to be infants in so many ways. As if they had just been born.

Nike Corp headquarters was fourteen city blocks large. They owned almost another twenty around that. The properties reached up the standard 400 stories. The space shuttle race was on and they would be the first to build. A giant checkmark would be seen on the face of the moon by every man, woman, and child from the quarter moon to full. The other corporations were lining up after to be next. The companies really didn't have to advertise because they buy the programmed birthing rites. Programming the infants: Coco-cola baby, Best Buy baby, Apple baby. Amazon will deliver a baby straight to your uterus in six weeks. Two months for Babies-R-Us showers and then birth in four. The machines take over, and it's straight to the incubators. Sponsored incubators and preemie of course. No one wants stretch marks. But the growth rate is strong. And don't like your baby? We'll ship it straight to the stem cell harvesting plant (return shipping not included). All this for the low-low price of product programming.

"They can boycott us, the next generation will buy us out," Nike's CEO said at the press conference addressing the buying drop. "The robot builders will succeed. Their programs run themselves. It seems we may have a new wave of second class citizens, but they will come around." He concluded by announcing the date for the construction launch.

The computers first picked up the buying anomaly in the Northwest quadrant. Something just wasn't right. Unexplained fluctuations in the buying codes. Just a flicker at first, then a massive trough in the charts. Citizens weren't buying like they were programmed. There was no protocol for anyone breaking the mind melds. It had never been done before. Ehud had just figured out how to do it. And then just figured how to unlock others. And then just figured how to build a bomb. And then just figured how to put it in the building.

On the day of the attack the news didn't even flash up. Instead a perfectly blonde programmed man-baby reaffirmed the code that led and brought comfort. "Government is business. Business is government. We buy for business. We buy for government. We buy ourselves."

The Black Hoods overrode the feed and cut in with a speech from Ehud. He stood in silence for a few seconds, his weathered face filling the frame. "I was the first to break programming. The first to reclaim choice. I couldn't have done it without her. She changed my thinking. The naked moon called to me and I had to answer. She is my muse. She could be yours, or your children's, or your children's children, as well. But you'll never hear the call lit from a billboard. We'll fight you until the end. We'll tear down the whole universe if it means keeping property from your hands. The choice now becomes yours. Goodnight and goodbye."

The feed cut to silent pictures of the bare lit moon before switching to live footage of the rebellion. Black Hoods swarmed the buildings like ants. Viewers began fighting their minds because personal revolution thoughts were never programmed. And these fighters on the screen weren't second-class. The last of those had been rounded up. These were first class citizens, bringing shock to a nation beyond shock. Thousands and thousands of the Nine Hoods swept into the buildings with bombs. A kamikaze wave, the buildings began falling all around. Ehud was singled out among them and snatched up by the robot police. His backpack detonated in the air, exploding the flying craft and all inside, raining a shower of hot metal and debris amidst the chaos. The last thing the news feed showed before being cut was the construction shuttle lifting off to the moon as the factories collapsed down.

81. She Loves Me

My knuckles, bloody, bruised and smiling,
    take down empires,
and rebuild walls (that look just
                    like you).

82. The Lifting Wind

Karen killed Thomas with a dull knife. It hadn't been sharpened in years, but it slid in deep. She pulled it out without breaking eye contact and thrust it in four more times. So much quieter than the pistol, and so much more personal. She left his body where it fell even though by that point he had technically lost possession and she went to the park to fly a kite. She stood looking at the sky and very little troubled her mind. Blood covered her shirt, splattered on her neck. Her tiny leather shoes were caked in mud.

"Come here kid," she said.

The boy must have been ten or so. He trembled but held the kite up. Karen walked backwards and let out enough string but still kept it tight.

"Alright hold it up high," she yelled.

The boy stood on his tiptoes. "Now throw it up."

The kid heaved with all his might. The string held tight and snapped in the wind. Karen deftly allowed the string to fly from her fingers and the kite weaved back and forth, up and up. She let out about 100 feet, stood, and stared. She grasped the back of her neck, slid her hand around and down and pushed her breast sideways, letting out a long sigh. Her head stayed back and her eyes didn't leave the kite as all the tightness melted from her body. The little boy walked carefully over to her.

"Are you okay?"

"Why you say that?" she didn't take her eyes off the kite dancing in the wind.

"You got blood on you."

"Well it isn't mine, mostly."

"Who's is it?" he shifted from one foot to the other.

"Nobody's now."

"You're good with that kite," he said.

"Thanks."

"You mind if I take a turn. I'm small but I'm strong."

"Me too, kid, me too." She handed it to him. Sirens started up in the background. "We might need to set that kite loose."

"You want a turn again?"

"Nah I'm free now." They stood looking up, as the sirens got louder.

She pulled the old dull broken blade and quickly sliced the string. The kite sailed on and away.

"Kid don't ever forget today. Things on the inside have a way of coming out. Things tethered fly away." Karen folded the knife and stuck it in her jeans. She lay down in the grass, kicked off her dirty shoes, and went to sleep. The kid watched her for a couple minutes and then walked off across the park.

83. Young Love is the Dumbest Love

He cycled the old Honda motorcycle up to fourth gear and
held steady on the accelerator. The bike whined and the
wind blew past and the seat warmed his pants. The leaves
covered the road and the trees stood bare with their
plaintive fingers outstretched to the sleet gray sky. His
thoughts were not on the girl, or the wedding he was
racing towards. Only the road and vibrations came
through to his mind.

He leaned hard into a left turn and the bike tilted
over. The tires pressed deep into the pavement and the
bike and rider both become part of the circle. He felt at
once stable and perfectly weightless.

Her name was Mary. She had kink brown hair and a
slender frame. He normally went for girls with fuller
breasts and hips. This time it didn't seem to make much
difference though. She was marrying another man today,
and that was all that mattered. And on he raced to the
coast. His mind blank like sandstone.

The church was old and massive. A brick dinosaur in
the dead coastal town. He filed in amongst the family and
friends and sat quietly. He couldn't really focus on the
words or the service, as all around him the smell of
mothballs battered his nose. His brain screamed at him to
shout out, to wave his arms, to run up and stop the whole
thing. Was no one else going to say anything? Thoughts
battered his brain and he felt nauseous. But other's
happiness does not ask your permission, and he stayed
silent. Soon the ceremony was over. Everyone was filing
out. The groom shook his hand and said with a smile, "Be
glad it's not you." He hung his head and watched his
shoes take the steps down the church on their own
volition. He went straight to the reception, and proceeded

to get miserably drunk. And after that night he never saw her in person again.

84. Warm Summer Night

Like the peaceful sleeping whales.
I roll onto my back,
and lazily turn my gaze to the heavens.

85. Poppy

Poppy you didn't tell me it was going to be like this. You knew the whole time and didn't say a word. Or did you know? What secrets did you have buried in that old chest of yours. I saw you cry and felt my world was nothing. What could I have done? I wasn't like the others. The men who were men when no one showed them how. They came into it like a new pair of sneakers. They wear them out and the world bows down and that's that. And that's the fantasy if there ever was one. Sure some might have it easier with the money piled high and never saying I want to do that but can't find a way to pay. But they might have a tougher time seeing their souls or feeling the loss or fuck who gives a shit about some rich piece of pie somewhere I can't see that's not me. I'm here and I'm real and that's the mother-fucking gospel. If Jesus is coming back he better bring a couple real big guns.

I have to find my own voice and the rest will flow so seamless. Seamless like a punch to the mouth. You come up spitting blood and teeth and still you come up and square off time and again. I can't see the future and the past looks murky. I don't know if I can even see my own heart anymore through these muddy eyes. But this song makes me happy and these keys going clickity clackity make me happy. It's always 2:31 in the morning and there ain't no such thing as 2:32. It's all just an illusion and why my heart got so wrapped up in this time and the comparisons I might draw I have no idea. Just let it all out. Empty everything and the good things might come back.

Write a million words. Fuck Thomas Wolfe. Let him write 10,000 and go get drinks. I'll write a million and drink light from the stars. The challenge has been spotted. Let it all go and help others any way you can. Get them where they want to go. You want to die, Dr. K., here let me lend you a hand. Stay the positron in the middle. Line em up and let them flow. Wake early and burn late. Let the world go. Let the world go on. Let the world go. Let the world take itself. Sit and think and don't think and exist and live in that moment you have there. Stop comparing your bank to your brother's bank and your future to your brother's future. Or your sisters present or even your own past. There is some good and some bad but the path is my own and I must walk. If you want to walk next to me that's worth something but no one can carry you.

86. Birth of a Superhero

"The question is not does God exist but Does Satan?"
Josiah said. The two gangsters were hefting the body out
of the trunk. It was wrapped head to toe in black plastic
and tied with twine.

"Oof, this fucker is heavy. I swear everybody's
getting fatter. Back when I started guys was skinny," Tim
answered. 'Twoguns" was the thinnest bagman in the
business. 6'2" 160 lbs., quick as lighting and responsible
for more deaths every year. "Grab his feet. And what's
that matter for?"

Josiah grabbed the corpse's shoes and pulled. The
brown lace-ups came off in his hand. The body dropped
and he stumbled backwards. "Dammit," he muttered
angrily. Twoguns said nothing this time as a slight smile
creased his face. He continued to hold the head. Josiah
kicked the shoes out of the way before reaching down to
grab the legs again. They started shuffling towards the
water's edge.

"Well let's just say God exists. Did he create evil or
does evil naturally exist in him or did Satan create it? Or
did humans create it?" Josiah asked.

Twoguns took his time answering. "Maybe there is
no evil. Maybe we ascribe good and evil causes to neutral
events? Gottdam he's leaking brains onto my shoe, turn
him up."

The bag crinkled as they rolled it over. They resumed
slowly duck walking the body towards the pier. Twoguns
dropped his end and pulled an old metal lever hidden in
the rocks. The sound of metal grating broke the morning
quiet as a platform rose out of the river. Long chains were
attached to each side. "Got to make sure fat boy don't

float," Twoguns said. They hefted the body onto the platform and started roping the chains around.

"I guess a better way to look at it is if Satan doesn't exist then all evil is either from man or God." Josiah said.

Four gunshots burst out in quick succession. Twogun's jaw exploded as Josiah felt a hot fire searing into his stomach. He stumbled backwards and felt the same fire in his leg. He fell over the platform rail and sunk down with the body into the murky water. The trash of the East River slowly floated by and his eyes started to burn from the refuse. His blood drifted into the water and down with the current. He saw a demon gliding up from the depths to collect him. It came within inches of his face and stared at him with emerald eyes. Its emotionless face warped to let out a grin that seemed to wrap around the back of its head, showing fangs like glass razors. The corpse floated down past Josiah, and he saw cluster of demons rise from the dark and grab it from all sides. The emerald demon lightly scratched his leg wound with a dirty metal claw. The demon blinked and clicked his teeth together before turning to the man in the bag. Josiah swam back to the surface. The river had carried him about twenty feet from the platform. He popped up and his eyes broke the water like a submerged frog. He dove back under and swam to the bank. Hanging onto a large rock, he reached under his coat and pulled out a wet Glock Seven.

"There are no demons, only me," he whispers and waits. His eyes stay locked on the two men advancing on his partner.

87.   14 Seconds

The sailor looks for his friend but sees only an empty deck remains as the wave drags him overboard and into the sea. The freezing arctic water hits and envelops him like an astronaut in space. He fights to the surface but the waves are climbable towers. They wash over him and he sinks deeper every time. Two waves pass and he cannot see the boat. The water fills his boots and like an iron clamp he is held. His mouth fills with ice water and his teeth and lungs go numb. He fights to the surface once more before all his energy is gone. The sea thrashes over him and like an anchor he seeks the ocean floor. He can feel his bones through his skin.   Down into a blackness he hasn't experienced since the womb. An old whale senses an intruder in the yard and turns a lazy eye to the seaman. He knows he will soon be gone and with a flip of his fin turns away. The last thoughts of the sailor flash like lighting. He dreams of being wrapped in the old man's blubber, surrounded like a coat and living forever inside the whale. He wonders if whales prefer spending their time in the icy north or warm South Seas and why he never took the time to learn their migration patterns. He finds the bottom where crabs wait with upturned claws and eyes on sticks. He has pulled tens of thousands up in his short fishing life. His brain sparks random for the next thirty minutes as they cover his body and complete the circle.

88. Eighty eight

The bright chrome double barrel was inches from his face. Two perfect circles, a sideways eight. Blood flowed into his left eye and his sight became a little fuzzy. Then there were four circles. Double infinity, eighty-eight. He wasn't sure which barrel held his death. He tried to focus, cut it down to one gun, but the haze remained. His wife lay there in a gruesome pile and he wasn't sure of his children.

"Why this world," he thought, "the devil did exist." And like a comet shooting through space to seed a planet, buckshot left the gun faster than the speed of sound. And the tiny pellets knocked on his skin like little salesmen, let us come in, let us come in. And his skin welcomed them in as the world and all he knew, faded away.

The End

Last Word and the Girl
Love grows here,
Right at the end.

ABOUT THE AUTHOR

I 'm 33, and can't say I was born the king. I haven't always been the king, and probably won't ever be. But even when I've been thrown into the dirt with my face ground down, for some reason, I've always felt like the king.

www.ingramcontent.com/pod-product-compliance
Lightning Source LLC
Chambersburg PA
CBHW060500280326
41933CB00014B/2800